TEST YOUR BASEBALL IQ

Dom Forker
Illustrated by Sanford Hoffman

Sterling Publishing Co., Inc.   New York

☉ Foreword ☉

Test Your Baseball IQ is full of rule applications you've seldom seen—but very easily could. Whether you're a Little Leaguer, a high-school or semi-pro player, a college or professional minor-league athlete, a major leaguer, a coach or manager—or just anyone who enjoys following any or all of the above—you're going to enjoy this book and perhaps learn a little from it.

The next time you see all four umpires huddling to discuss a tricky play, you're going to be one step ahead of them. You're going to be able to tell your friends, "They're going to call the 'Compromise Rule,'" or, "They're going to call the 'Baseball Bluff Rule.'"

And you won't be bluffing!

Library of Congress Cataloging-in-Publication Data

Forker, Dom.
    Test your baseball IQ / by Dom Forker.
        p.   cm.
    Includes index.
    ISBN 0-8069-8802-9
    1. Baseball—Rules—Miscellanea.   2. Baseball—United States—
Rules—Miscellanea.   I. Title.
GV877.F595   1993
796.357'02'022—dc20   92–44925
                                       CIP

10   9

Published by Sterling Publishing Company, Inc.
387 Park Avenue South, New York, N.Y. 10016
© 1993 by Dom Forker
Distributed in Canada by Sterling Publishing
% Canadian Manda Group, P.O. Box 920, Station U
Toronto, Ontario, Canada M8Z 5P9
Distributed in Great Britain by Chrysalia Books
64 Brewery Road, London N7 9NT, England
Distributed in Australia by Capricorn Link (Australia) Pty, Ltd.
P.O. Box 704, Windsor, NSW 2756 Australia
Printed in China
All rights reserved

Sterling ISBN 0-8069-8802-9

☉ CONTENTS ☉

◎ Introduction ◎

This is the third book in a trilogy that tests your knowledge of the rules. The first, *Baseball Brain Teasers*, was first published in 1986 and *Big League Baseball Puzzlers* followed in 1991. In each book we have tried to unearth new applications to old rules, plays that either recently happened or could happen—any day now!

In this book we have Tommy LaSorda, the manager of the Los Angeles Dodgers, admitting that he didn't know that if a catcher (Mike Scioscia) fields a ball with his mask, there is a two-base penalty.

We also have four veterans with a total of approximately 150 years of major-league experience—both on the field and in the broadcast booth—say that before the 1992 season they had never known that a batter's request for a base umpire to move could be denied. Early in that year, Phillie batter Lenny Dykstra requested second-base umpire Joe West to move out of his line of vision. West refused to move.

In the fourth Met game of the season, Eddie Murray made the same request of second-base umpire Frank Pulli, who also denied the request. Late in the season, Murray *again* asked a second-base umpire (Terry Tata) to move, but once again he was turned down.

Phillie broadcasters, Harry Kallas and Richie Ashburn, couldn't believe that Dykstra's request was denied. Ashburn, who won two major-league batting titles, in 1955 and 1958, summed up their sentiments when he said, "What's the big deal? He (Dykstra) wasn't asking for a loan."

Met announcers, Tim McCarver and Ralph Kiner, both of whom were outstanding ballplayers, were just as flabbergasted when Murray's second request was ignored. Kiner said, "I don't know. He wasn't asking for a contract extension."

"Casey said it's my turn to bat."

◎ 1 ◎

LITTLE-KNOWN RULES

Sharing an At-Bat

Casey Stengel is playing with his batting order and alternating Phil Rizzuto and Billy Martin in the number-one and number-eight spots. On Friday he had Martin batting first and Rizzuto eighth. On Saturday Martin steps into the batter's box to begin the game at Briggs Stadium in Detroit. Tiger pitcher Hal Newhouser runs a count of no balls and two strikes on Martin before Rizzuto realizes *he* is the named lead-off batter for the Yankees for this game. The "Scooter" rushes up and takes Martin's place in the batter's box. On Newhouser's next pitch Rizzuto swings and misses.

Is anyone called out for batting out of order here? Who is charged with the strikeout?

*　*　*

Rizzuto, as the proper batter, gets charged with the strikeout. No one is called out for batting out of order. The proper batter may take his place in the batter's box at any time before the improper batter becomes a runner or is put out, and any balls and strikes shall be counted in the proper batter's time at bat. Rule 6.07 (a) (1).

Instant Replay

Can the instant replay camera cause a pitcher's ejection?

* * *

No, but it certainly created a furor during the 1992 season. Tim Leary, pitcher for the New York Yankees, got off to a bad start early in the season. Suddenly he righted himself with three consecutive victories toward the middle of June. Then, in defeating the host Orioles one night, he threw an errant pitch that broke Chris Hoiles's wrist. Johnny Oates, Baltimore's manager, was suspicious of the pitch that sidelined Hoiles. While the game continued, he began to collect the discarded balls and place them in a bucket. According to him, they were all defaced. When he had enough evidence, he presented the balls to the home-plate umpire.

The umpire, who didn't *have* to go out to the mound, did so anyway a few pitches later to search Leary. He found nothing! The diamond-vision camera on the center field scoreboard, however, detected Leary removing a substance—it was thought to be sandpaper—from his glove and putting it in his mouth. The umpire didn't see Leary do it. Oates, who saw it on the screen, asked the umpire to look in Leary's mouth. The umpire, who said it was beyond his authority, refused.

The next day the diamond-vision film excerpt was shown on television stations all over America. There was a demand for action on the part of the league office. President Bobby Brown called Leary in for a meeting, but he let him off with a warning.

Nothing in the rule book says an umpire's or league office's decision can be influenced by the view on an instant replay camera.

After the incident Leary was no longer effective with the Yankees, though, and in late August he and his huge ERA were shipped to the Mariners.

The House Call

A pitcher for a Western Division team in the American League and a hurler for an Eastern Division club in the National League are both caught doctoring the ball. The first moundsman is found to be hiding an emery board in his back pocket, and the second one is caught with sandpaper attached to his glove.

If you're the umpire-in-chief, how do you resolve the scratchy situation?

*   *   *

The umpires in the case of Joe Niekro of the 1987 Minnesota Twins and Kevin Gross of the 1987 Phillies ejected both pitchers from their respective games. In addition, their respective league presidents tacked on ten-day suspensions. Rule 3.02, PENALTY.

Pine Tar Two

George Brett was not the only player to gain notoriety from a pine-tar incident. Jay Howell, the pitcher, did, too.

When Howell came on in relief in the 1988 National League Championship Series, Met manager Davey Johnson asked home-plate umpire Joe West to check the pitcher's glove. West called for Harry Wendelstedt, the crew chief of the umpire unit, to help him inspect the glove. Wendelstedt put his hand in the glove and his hand stuck to it. The heel of the glove was covered with pine tar.

Do you remember how the National League handled the previous sensitive situation? You might remember that no prior player had been banned from a National League playoff game for using an illegal substance on the ball.

*   *   *

Wendelstedt ejected Howell from the game. The rule book explicitly says that if a pitcher has pine tar or any foreign substance on him, he is to be ejected. Then-National League President A. Bartlett Giamatti issued a three-day suspension to Howell. He later reduced the ban to two games. Rule 3.02 PENALTY.

Something to Balk About

The Cardinals have runners on second and third base after Vince Coleman doubles Ozzie Smith to third base. Then the Atlanta Braves pitcher balks Smith home and Coleman to third base. Before the next pitch, however, the Braves first baseman calls for the ball, steps on first base, and claims that Coleman missed that base while running out his double.

The umpire saw Coleman miss the base. How should he rule?

* * *

He should deny the appeal. Even though no pitch had been made since Coleman's double, the rule states that an appeal must be made before the "next pitch or any play or attempted play." The balk constitutes a play. Rule 7.10 d, paragraph beginning "Any appeal."

The Trial Run

A Milwaukee Brewer relief pitcher comes into a game to face Cecil Fielder of the Tigers in the bottom of the seventh inning. Before the new hurler throws the first of his eight warm-up pitches, he spits on his hands. The home-plate umpire calls, "Ball one," and warns the pitcher not to do it again.

But the Brewer hurler defies the umpire and spits on his hands again before he throws his second warm-up pitch. The umpire then ejects the pitcher. Brewer manager Phil Garner, who argued the first call from the bench, now charges the plate umpire and hotly contests the first and second calls.

Does Garner have the rule book on his side?

* * *

Today he does. But if the incident had happened before the 1969 season, he wouldn't. In fact, it was a situation in 1968 that prompted league officials to amend this rule.

In a game at Shea Stadium, John Boozer of the Phillies came into the contest in the bottom of the seventh inning to replace Woody Fryman. Before Boozer took his first warm-up pitch, he spat on his hands. Plate umpire Ed Vargo called, "Ball one."

At this point Phillie manager Gene Mauch charged out of the Philadelphia dugout and ordered Boozer to repeat his act. Boozer did. Vargo, who could have ejected Boozer there, called, "Ball two." Mauch insisted that Boozer repeat his ritual. The pitcher did—and was promptly ejected by Vargo. Several minutes later, Mauch was ejected, too. The three ball calls stood. Dick Hall came into the game—with a 3-0 count—to pitch to Met batter Buddy Harrelson.

Mauch lost the argument but he won a point by bringing attention to a foolish rule in the book. After the season it was removed. The rules committee voted to exclude warm-ups from the rule.

Nothing to Feel Blue About

Vida Blue had a big year in his rookie season with the 1971 Oakland A's. He won 24 games and lost just 8 while leading the league in ERA (1.82) and shutouts (8). In addition, he struck out 301 batters to become the only pitcher to fan 300 or more hitters in a rookie season. For his scintillating efforts, he was named the league's MVP.

Charlie Finley, colorful owner of the A's, asked Blue after the 1971 season if he would change his first name from "Vida" to "True" so that the two names would rhyme and they would have a *double entendre* effect.

Blue refused. But one day he walked out on the mound with a glove that was colored blue. He said that he wanted his name and his glove to be uniform.

Was there anything wrong with that?

* * *

No. It can be blue, but it cannot be white or gray. Otherwise, the glove, including the stitching, lacing, and webbing, must be uniform in color. Rule 1.15 (a).

In fact, Vida wore a blue glove for most of his career.

The Quick Pitch

Reggie Jackson used to take a lot of time to get ready in the batter's box. In this hypothetical situation, he is still a Yankee, and he is batting with a three-two count with no one on base against a crafty Red Sox hurler.

The BoSox pitcher fires a strike right down the middle of the plate before Jackson is set, but the umpire calls it a quick pitch.

What's the penalty?

* * *

The umpire calls the pitch a ball. That makes four on Jackson, so he goes to first base. Rule 8.05 (e).

* * *

Would there have been a ball call if there had been runners on base? No, it would have been a balk. A runner at third would score, a runner at first would go to second, etc. Reggie would remain at the plate with a three-two count. Rule 8.05 (e).

* * *

It happened in the fourth and final game of the 1928 World Series, Bill Sherdel of the Cardinals "slipped" a third strike by Babe Ruth, but plate umpire Charles Pfirman disallowed the offering, calling it a quick pitch. A ball was added to the Babe's count, and then Ruth hit his third home run of the game (for the second time in World Series play). All of his homers that day were solo shots.

A Fine Line

The Phillies have Dale Sveum, Lenny Dykstra, and John Kruk on third, second, and first bases, respectively, when Dale Murphy rips a line drive back at the opposing pitcher with one out. The pitcher drops the ball, picks it up, and then initiates a pitcher-to-home-to-first double play to end the inning.

Or does he?

*   *   *

There is a fine line in this situation. It's a judgment call on the part of the umpire. He has to determine whether the pitcher purposefully or accidentally dropped the ball.

*   *   *

On May 20, 1960, the exact same play that is described above happened in a game between the Reds and the Cardinals. Joe Nuxhall was the pitcher for the Reds; Stan Musial the batter for the Cardinals. Umpire Ed Vargo ruled that Nuxhall dropped the ball on purpose. Remember, no infield fly rule can be called on a line drive. Musial was declared out and the ball dead, and the umpire ordered the runners to return to their original bases. Rule 6.05 (L).

Snap Throw

There are many present-day left-handed pitchers who come to a set position with a runner on first, step back off the pitcher's rubber with their pivot foot, and without a step toward first base throw to first base.

Legal play?

* * *

Yes, provided that the pitcher's pivot foot, in stepping back, touches the ground before he separates his hands. Rule 8.01 (E).

* * *

Dave Righetti, when he used to pitch with the Yankees, was one of the pitchers who popularized this move.

"Why can't he pitch it straight?"

How High Can a Pitch Go?

Is there any height limit to the trajectory of a hurler's pitch?

* * *

No, the rule book doesn't cover the subject. Truett "Rip" Sewell of the 1943 Pirates was delighted to find that out. One day during the season, he became the first major-league pitcher to throw a lob to the plate. Some viewers said that the pitch rose almost thirty feet above the ground.

Sewell had a number of other pitches that were effective: fastball, curveball, slider, forkball, and change-up. In fact, he posted a league-leading 21 wins that season. But he wanted the hitter to be thinking of his "eephus pitch." It helped to set up some of his other pitches.

Sewell frustrated National League hitters for four years with the lob pitch. None of them ever hit it for a home run. One day Eddie Miller of the Reds was so frustrated that he caught the pitch and fired it back to Sewell. The home-plate umpire called that pitch a strike.

There's a climax. It occurred in the 1946 All-Star Game, which the American League won, 12-0. In that game Ted Williams hit two home runs and drove home five runs in his home stadium, Fenway Park. One of his home runs came against Sewell's "eephus pitch." Williams had thought about the possibility of seeing the pitch before the game. He concluded that the only way anyone could hit the ball out of the park was by running up on it. When he faced Sewell, he guessed right on the pitch, ran up on it, and with his feet in the batter's box timed it perfectly. The ball sailed deep into the right-center field bleachers for a home run—the first and only one that was ever hit off Sewell's "eephus pitch."

How high can a pitch go? Williams proved that it could go very high.

The Pitcher's Mound

How high above the base lines and home plate is the pitcher's mound?

*   *   *

Ten inches.

*   *   *

Has it always been that height in the 20th century?

*   *   *

No, it has evolved over time. In 1903 it was established that the mound should not be more than 15 inches above the base lines and home plate. In 1950 the height of the mound was fixed at 15 inches above the base lines and home plate. Finally, in 1968 the mound was lowered to 10 inches above the base lines and home plate, where it remains today. Rule 1.07.

*   *   *

The reason that the mound was lowered in the 1969 season was because of the pitchers' dominance in 1968. That year the top ERA mark in the National League belonged to Bob Gibson (1.12). And Bob Bolin (1.99), Bob Veale (2.05), Jerry Koosman (2.08), and Steve Blass (2.12) rounded out the top five.

In the American League the top five ERA's belonged to Luis Tiant (1.60), Sam McDowell (1.81), Dave McNally (1.95), Denny McLain (1.96), and Tommy John (1.98).

That was also the year that McLain won 31 games. For the first time in 34 years, a pitcher won 30 games in a season. No one has won 30 games in a year since 1968.

Also, in 1968, Don Drysdale pitched a record six consecutive shutouts and spun a then-record 58 and two-thirds consecutive scoreless innings.

Simply put, the fans wanted to see scoring and excitement—not low-hit games and strikeouts!

How Close Can "The Barber" Throw?

Sal Maglie, pitcher with the New York Giants in the early 1950s, was called "The Barber," for two reasons. One was because he didn't shave on the day of a game, and he had a heavy dark beard. The second was because his pitches "shaved" the heads of opposing hitters, especially those of the Brooklyn Dodgers.

Quite often the Dodger players suspected that Maglie's "purpose pitches" were signalled by Giant (skipper) Leo Durocher, who managed the Dodgers from 1939 to 1948. Dodger fans and players had a love-hate relationship with Durocher.

Let us hypothesize that in 1954 Maglie knocked down slugger Gil Hodges three straight times. Then, with the winning run on second base and two out in the bottom of the ninth inning at Ebbets Field he threw so close to Hodges' head that he had to fall to the ground.

Would Maglie have been ejected from the game? Would Durocher have been thrown out, also?

* * *

Probably not. The plate umpire undoubtedly would have warned the pitcher and turned in a report to the league office, which would have resulted in a fine being levied against him. Durocher may or may not have been fined, also. Rules 9.01 (d) and 9.05 (a).

But umpires and head-hunting pitchers got away with much more in those days than they do today. Dizzy Dean of the Cardinals, for example, once knocked down eight consecutive Giant batters in the mid-1930s.

Back in the 1950s, hitters were supposed to retaliate with their own methods. One summer afternoon in 1956, when Maglie was pitching *for* the Dodgers *against* the Giants, "The Barber" knocked Willie Mays down on two consecutive pitches. The umpire warned Maglie, who defended himself by saying that "my fingers were sweating and the balls just slipped out."

"Tell Willie I'm sorry," Maglie said to the plate umpire.

Willie hit the next pitch for a long home run. As Mays circled the bases, he delivered his own "knockdown" to Maglie, when he told the third base umpire, "Tell Sal I'm sorry."

The Trick That Backfired

The hidden-ball trick has to be done just right in order for it to work. It also has to be done correctly to avoid a balk being called. Take the following case, for example.

On August 12, 1961, San Francisco Giant shortstop Jose Pagan decided that he was going to pull the hidden-ball trick when Cincinnati catcher Johnny Edwards was on second base. He hid the ball in his glove and waited for Edwards to step off the base.

In the meantime, pitcher Jack Sanford strode to the mound, pretending that he had the ball. The second-base umpire was on the ball, though. He called a balk against Sanford. Why?

* * *

The pitcher, without the ball, cannot stand either on or astride the mound. Rule 8.05 (i).

* * *

In *Baseball Brain Teasers*, we referred to a more celebrated case, when Dick Groat of the Cardinals, in the fourth game of the 1964 World Series, pulled the hidden-ball trick against Mickey Mantle of the Yankees at second base. That play worked because Roger Craig, the Redbird pitcher, fiddled in the playing area off the pitcher's mound before and during the time that Groat applied the tag.

Pitch-O-Meters

Dennis Cook, a notoriously slow worker, is the pitcher for the Indians in a game in which Cleveland holds a 3-2 lead over the Blue Jays in the top half of the seventh inning. There are two out, no one on base, and Joe Carter is up at the plate with a full count on him. Cook shakes off a couple of signs, backs off the rubber, looks at his outfield alignment, gets back on the rubber, and stares interminably at the batter. All of a sudden, the plate umpire jumps out from behind the plate and calls, "Ball four."

Can the plate umpire do that?

*   *   *

Rule 8.04 says he can. The pitcher must deliver the ball to the hitter, when the bases are unoccupied, within 20 seconds after he gets the ball. Each violation of this rule will result in a ball call.

*   *   *

The 20-second rule is rarely called. The umpire just has too many things to do to count to 20 seconds or consult a watch. However, if the pitcher is a notoriously slow worker, the umpire might decide to clock the hurler.

Joe Cronin, when president of the American League, decided to get tough on 1969 pitchers who stalled on the mound. He told each club that it had to install a "pitch-o-meter" on the scoreboard. But most clubs balked. Only the Indians and White Sox went along with his edict. Soon the crackdown subsided. It went the way of most baseball fads, as, for example, get-tough policies on pitchers who balk.

"Watch out when I take a big swing."

Batter's Interference?

The Cincinnati batter, trying to protect Barry Larkin, who is running from first on the pitch, swings at Phillie pitcher Terry Mulholland's offering. His big swing misses, but his bat comes all the way around and hits Darren Daulton in the head just after he has released the ball on his throw to second base. Nevertheless, Daulton manages to throw Larkin out.

In another incident Mackay Sasser of the 1992 Mets got a bloody nose when a Pirate batter, Barry Bonds, hit Sasser's nose on his back swing.

Was the batter called out in these cases?

No. If the batter had interfered with the catcher's fielding or throwing by stepping out of the batter's box or making any other movement which hinders or impedes the catcher's play, he is out. Also, he is out if the umpire thinks his act is intentional. However, the batter is not out if any runner who is attempting to advance is thrown out. Rule 6.06 (c) EXCEPTION.

If Larkin had reached second safely, the batter would have been called out.

* * *

In May of 1986 there was an enactment of this play. The Yankees, who were playing the Rangers, had Henry Cotto at the plate and Gary Roenicke at first. Roenicke was running on the pitch, Cotto swung through the pitch and hit

"Don't squat so near me, buddy."

catcher Don Slaught, who was attempting to throw the runner out, in the head. Slaught's throw sailed into center field, and Roenicke raced to third on the play.

In this case, Cotto was called out on batter's interference, and Roenicke was returned to first base. The ball became dead as soon as the interference took place. Rule 6.06 (c).

Double Penalty

An Oakland A's batter is at the plate in the top half of the seventh inning with two out, a three-two count, and the bases loaded. Just as the Mariner pitcher is about to go into his wind-up, the batter steps out of the box and requests the umpire for time-out. The arbiter doesn't give it to him! The pitcher pitches. Scott Bradley, the Seattle catcher, has to jump to prevent the pitch from sailing for a wild pitch.

What happens next?

* * *

The pitch, though wild, is called an automatic strike, the batter is out, and the inning is over. The umpire doesn't *have* to give the batter time-out if he feels that it was requested too late or for the wrong reason. It is the batter's responsibility to know whether the time-out has been granted. Rule 6.02 (b) and (c).

* * *

Jose Canseco of the A's got called out on such a play during the 1992 season.

Leaning Over the Plate

Minnie Minoso of the White Sox liked to lean over the plate. (He led the major leagues in career hit-by-pitches until Don Baylor later broke the mark.)

One day during the hot-and-steamy summer of 1955, Minoso was leaning over the plate when he was hit with a three-two pitch in the strike zone by Whitey Ford of the Yankees.

Did the umpire give Minoso a hit-by-pitch award or a walk or neither?

* * *

He gave him neither. Instead, he invoked Rule 6.08 (b) against him: "If the ball is in the strike zone when it touches the batter, it shall be called a strike, whether or not the batter tries to avoid the ball."

* * *

Suppose in the same situation Minoso got hit by the pitch when he was standing six inches off the plate. Would it count as a hit-by-pitch or a walk?

* * *

A walk.

The Checked Swing

The visiting Braves are playing the Mets at Shea Stadium. Atlanta's John Smoltz is pitching to Vince Coleman, the New York center fielder. With two strikes on him, Coleman checks his swing on a borderline pitch. Plate umpire Gary Darling calls the pitch a ball, but catcher Greg Olson appeals the call.

The plate umpire asks third-base umpire Dana DeMuth for his angle on the swing. DeMuth signals that the batter swung at the pitch. Strikeout. Coleman then engages in a heated argument with DeMuth. Darling, who is a spectator to the argument, eventually throws Coleman out of the game.

Can he do this?

* * *

Yes, he can. The home-plate umpire is the umpire-in-chief.

* * *

Afterwards, Terry Pendleton, the Brave third baseman and a friend of Coleman's, said, "I don't know why Darling even threw him out. He [Coleman] was arguing with the third-base ump. Darling should have no authority to throw him out."

Only the authority of being the umpire-in-chief.

The Sultan's Bat

The *Official Baseball Rules* specifies that no bat can be longer than 42 inches or more than 2¾ inches in diameter. Rule 1.10 (a). Does it also limit the weight of the bat?

*   *   *

No, it doesn't.

*   *   *

Hack Miller of the 1922–23 Cubs claimed he used a 65-ounce bat. In those two seasons, the only ones in which he had a sufficient number of at-bats, he batted .352 and .301, respectively. In 1923 he hit a career-high 20 homers.

Babe Ruth, the "Sultan of Swat," at times used a 52-ounce bat, and he, of course, batted .342 lifetime and hit 714 career home runs.

Babe Herman, a .324 lifetime hitter, swung a 48-ounce bat during his heyday of 1928–30, when he batted .340, .381, and .393, respectively, for the Brooklyn Dodgers.

A Brooklyn teammate once asked Herman, "Why do you swing such a heavy bat?"

The Babe, known for his quick rejoinders, snapped, "If it's good enough for one Babe [Ruth], it's good enough for another Babe [Herman]."

Herman hit a career-high 35 home runs in 1930.

"How much your bat weigh, Willie?"

The Flea-Swatter's Bat

Most modern-day players swing bats that are much lighter than the lumberjacks of the 1920s and 1930s.

Richie Allen was an exception. He used a 42-ounce war club. But it worked for him. He won two home run titles (1972 and 1974) and one MVP Award (1972) with the White Sox. Career-wise, he batted .292 and hit 351 home runs, including a personal-high 40 homers with the 1966 Phillies.

But Willie Mays and Mickey Mantle used bats that were in the 32–34 ounce range. Mays hit 660 career homers; Mantle, 534.

Stan Musial swung a 31-ounce bat. "The Man" believed that the key variables were pitch speed and bat speed. Musial batted .331 and hit 475 home runs during his 22-year career. Along the way, he won seven batting crowns.

Today Tony Gwynn uses a 31-ounce bat. Going into the 1992 season, Gwynn was a .328 lifetime hitter. He had also won four batting titles.

But neither Musial nor Gwynn swung the lightest bat in baseball history. Can you name the Hall-of-Famer who did?

*   *   *

"Wee Willie" Keeler. The 5-4½, 140-pound outfielder, swung a flea-swatter bat, in "hitting them where they ain't," primarily for the Baltimore Orioles and the Brooklyn Dodgers, Keeler batted .343 lifetime, won two batting titles, hit .400 once (.424 for the 1897 Orioles), and collected 200 or more hits for eight consecutive (1894–1901) seasons.

Bat Color

Ball players are superstitious about many things, some about their bat. Babe Ruth used a black bat that he called "Black Betsy." It was his special home run stick. George Foster used black bats, too. They helped him to hit 52 home runs in 1977. Bats like the ones he used are known to have a "Foster Finish."

Tan bats that have a light stain are said to have the "Hornsby Finish." They were named after Rogers Hornsby, who used them en route to compiling a .358 lifetime batting average.

Two-tone bats are modeled after the ones that Harry "The Hat" Walker used. Walker won a batting title in 1947.

These natural shades are allowed. Are there any shades that are disallowed?

* * *

No colored bat may be used in a professional game unless it has been previously approved by the Rules Committee. Rule 1.10 (d).

* * *

There are exceptions to every rule, though. In 1947 Jerome "Dizzy" Dean was broadcasting baseball games for the St. Louis Browns, who were having their typical dismal season—both in the league standings and at the gate. For the Browns' final game of the season at Sportsman's Park, management asked Dean to suit up and pitch three innings. Always happy to provide a lark, Dizzy willingly went along with the gimmick to lure 20,000 or more paying customers to the park.

Six years after he had officially retired, he pitched three scoreless and hitless innings. He also went one-for-one at the plate. (During his career he batted .225 and hit eight home runs.) The *color* of the bat he used that day was red, white, and blue. Up until the end the Diz was "colorful."

One additional story of bat shades comes to the author's mind. When he was a teen-ager, he and his family were listening to a Phillie-Pirate game on the radio. Going into the bottom of the tenth inning, the score was tied, 1-1. Suddenly the Philadelphia broadcaster got excited. He gushed, "Uh-oh, Ralph Kiner's coming to the plate, and he's carrying his black bat with him. That's his special bat, his home run bat. That's the one he uses when he wants to end the game."

It was hard to believe that the announcer actually thought the shade of Kiner's bat could dictate the outcome of the game, as though it were some sort of talisman. But two pitches later, Kiner hit a ball over the roof in left field to end the game! It could make one a "true believer" overnight.

The Evasive Runner

The Cubs have Andre Dawson on third base and Ryne Sandberg on first base with two out. Shawon Dunston, the batter, hits a high-hopper near the second-base bag. Jose Oquendo of the Cardinals charges the ball and reaches out to tag Sandberg, who evades the tag by leaving the base path. The second-base umpire calls Sandberg out, but not before Dawson scores.

Does the run count?

* * *

No. Sandberg was forced. No run can score on a third out that is made on a force play. Rule 4.09 a—EXCEPTION: a run is not scored if the runner advances to home base during a play in which the third out is made by any runner being forced out.

Twice Out on One Play

Can one player be called out twice on the same play?

* * *

No, but it has happened. One day, umpire Nick Bremigan was working third base with a three-man crew in the minor leagues, when one of the teams loaded the bases with no out. The next batter hammered a hard ground ball to the third baseman, who stepped on the bag for the force out, and then fired the ball home to the catcher, who tagged the sliding runner for the second out.

In the meantime, the runner from second base (who had already been forced out at third) rounded third base and scrambled back, not realizing he had been forced out. Bremigan, who had made the initial call at third, positioned himself for a possible play on the runner from first, who might be trying to advance to third on the play. When the catcher fired the ball to the third baseman, Bremigan called the scrambling runner out—for the second time!

It should be noted that if the batter or a runner continues to advance after he has been put out, he shall not by that act alone be considered as confusing, hindering, or impeding the fielders. Rule 7.09 (7).

The Way the Ball Bounces

On August 22, 1992, Charlie Hayes of the Yankees, with no runners on base in a scoreless tie, hit a pitch by Chuck Finley of the Angels high and far down the left-field line at Yankee Stadium. The ball hit the "wire netting extending along the side of the pole on fair territory above the fence to enable the umpires more accurately to judge fair and foul balls" and rebounded to left fielder Luis Polonia in fair territory.

Did the third-base umpire rule the hit a foul ball, a home run, a double, or a ball that was still in play?

* * *

A home run. Today the foul poles in all major-league parks are placed in fair territory, behind the fence or wall. Thus, any batted ball that hits either the foul pole or the wire netting extending from it is a home run. Rule 2.00 A FAIR BALL.

Consequently, Hayes's hit, a solo home run, gave the Yankees a 1-0 lead in a game that they ultimately won, 3-0.

However, the foul poles at major league parks were not always placed behind either the fence or wall. They were once situated in a groove or hollow that was inserted into the top of the fence or wall. If the batted ball, at that time, struck the foul pole and bounded into the stands in foul territory, the batter was awarded a two-base hit; if the batted ball hit the foul pole and bounced over the fence in fair territory, the batter was awarded a home run; if the batted ball rebounded off the foul pole onto the playing field, the batter had to run out his hit. It was in-play.

Quite a Lark

In a late August 1992 game at Riverfront Stadium, in a game between the visiting Phillies and the Reds, Cincinnati's Barry Larkin hit a Pat Williams pitch deep to left field. The ball hit the top of the fence just above the yellow line, which is simply an aid to the umpires to judge whether the ball in flight truly cleared the fence. Then it bounced just slightly forward, grazing the tarpaulin that extends from the rear edge of the fence to the bottom edge of the lower grandstands that reside behind the fence, then bounced once again on the top of the fence, and then rebounded to the Phillie left fielder in fair territory.

What was the ruling?

*   *   *

Larkin was awarded a home run. The yellow line had nothing to do with the ruling. It was just a visual aid for the umpires. The tarpaulin, which was placed in home-run territory, was the determinating factor.

The Foxy Runner

While an improper batter (hitting out of turn) is at the plate for the Cardinals, the runner at first steals both second and third bases. When the improper batter ends up walking, the opposing manager appeals to the umpire before the first pitch is thrown to the following player, pointing out that the hitter batted out of turn.

Is the batter-runner called out?

* * *

No. The proper batter is called out. Rule 6.07 (a).

* * *

Does the runner have to return to first base?

* * *

No. If a runner advances, while the improper batter is at bat, on a stolen base, balk, wild pitch, or passed ball, such advance is legal. Rule 6.07 (b) NOTE.

* * *

The above situation happened to the Detroit Tigers in 1909. The Tigers won the American League pennant that year for the third season in a row. It just shows that even the best of teams can sometimes make mistakes.

With Ty Cobb at first base, left fielder Davy Jones improperly batted in Sam Crawford's place. Crawford was subsequently called out, but not before Cobb had picked up two stolen bases.

Swinging Third Strike

One of the most famous plays in baseball history took place in the bottom of the ninth inning of Game Three of the 1941 World Series. The Brooklyn Dodgers, down to the Yankees two games to one, were leading, 4-3, with two out and no one on base. Tommy Henrich was the batter for New York; Hugh Casey was the pitcher for Brooklyn. The count ran to three-and-two on Henrich. Then Casey broke off a hard curve—some said it was a spitter—and Henrich swung and missed. The game would have been over—but the ball got away from catcher Mickey Owen and rolled back to the screen, as Henrich ran safely to first base.

Then the roof fell in on Brooklyn. Joe DiMaggio singled and Charlie Keller doubled two runs home. After Bill Dickey walked, Joe Gordon doubled two more runs across the plate. The Yankees ended up winning the game, 7-4. When Henrich swung and missed, it appeared that Brooklyn had tied the Series at two games apiece. Instead, the Yankees held a commanding three-game-to-one lead. The next day the Yankees won, 3-1, and wrapped up a Series they very well could have lost.

In retrospect, though, wasn't Henrich's swinging strike the third out of the inning and the final out of the game?

* * *

No. To conclude a strikeout, the catcher must hold the third strike or pick up the loose ball and throw it to first base before the runner for the out to count. Henrich was safe at first base because he reached it before the throw. Rule 6.09 (b).

A No-Wynn Situation

Hal Morris of the Reds is at the plate with one out and a teammate on third base. Before the Pirate pitcher releases his next pitch, he balks, but Morris lines a drive off center fielder Andy Van Slyke's glove for a double. The runner at third starts for home on the play, but when he sees that Van Slyke has a possible play on the ball, he returns to third. When Van Slyke doesn't catch the ball, Morris tags and starts for home again. However, the Pittsburgh outfielder makes a quick recovery and throws to the plate while the runner retreats to third.

Red manager Lou Piniella comes out of the dugout after the play and tells the plate umpire he is waiving the balk call. He wants to take the play instead. But the umpire says he can't.

Why?

*   *   *

In order for the play to supersede the balk, all runners who were on base had to advance at least one base. Rule 8.05 (m) PENALTY. The runner at third would score on the balk, but Morris would have to come back to the plate and try all over again.

*   *   *

In April 1977, Jimmy Wynn of the Yankees was the runner at third base, and Lou Piniella was the hitter. Jerry Garvin of the Blue Jays was the pitcher with two out in the bottom of the fourth inning. Piniella "doubled" off the center fielder's glove, but Wynn didn't score on the play. He did score on Garvin's balk, though, while Piniella had to be tossed out of the game before he would give up second base and the double he had hit. Piniella's replacement struck out, and the Yankees went on to lose both the game and their protest.

You've Got to Run 'em Out

In a 1992 game between the White Sox and the host Yankees, New York's Randy Velarde singles to right field, a run scoring on the play. Dan Pasqua's relay throw misses the cut-off man, however, and Velarde continues on to second base on the play.

When catcher Carlton Fisk realizes that there is no White Sox teammate backing up the play, he races to retrieve the ball as it rolls toward the visitors' third-base dugout. At the last possible second, he slides feet-first into the dugout in order to stop and recover the ball. Ultimately, he takes firm possession of the ball, which had come to rest on the top step of the dugout.

Velarde, who thinks that the ball has gone into dead territory, and that he is entitled to a free base, trots to third base, but Fisk now steps out of the dugout and throws the ball to third baseman Robin Ventura for an easy tag-out.

The Yankees don't protest the call. Should they have?

* * *

No. A fielder or catcher may reach or step into, or go into, the dugout with one or both feet to make a catch (play), and if he holds the ball, the catch (play) shall be allowed. The ball is in play. Rule 7.04 (c).

Double Play on a Triple

This unusual play probably won't ever be duplicated. It occurred in a game between the Philadelphia Athletics and the Cleveland Indians during World War II. The Tribe had Oris Hockett on first base when Lou Boudreau, the Indians' playing manager, hit a rocket to the right-center field wall.

Hockett thought he would score on the play, but the relay throw to the plate beat him by at least 20 feet. The Cleveland runner, knowing that he would be an easy out at the plate, decided to get into a rundown, so he retreated to third. But Boudreau by that time was standing safely on the bag. So Hockett inexplicably walked past third and headed toward his position in left field. Buddy Rosar, the Athletic catcher, alertly ran after and tagged Hockett, as well as Boudreau, who was still standing on the base.

Philadelphia's manager, Connie Mack, insisted that the Athletics should get two outs on the play. Did he get them?

* * *

Not initially. The third-base umpire called Hockett out, but he ruled that Boudreau was safe. Mack pointed out that since Hockett had retreated beyond Boudreau, the Indian manager should be called out for passing a base runner, and since Hockett had abandoned his base path, he should be called out, too. Mack turned on the light switch for the umpire, who agreed with him. Double play. Rules 7.08 (a) and (b).

The Best-Laid Plans

The Pirates have runners at first and second, with one out, and their number-three man is at the plate. Manager Jim Leyland flashes the double-steal sign, but the runner at first initially misses it and gets a late start. The batter, out of the corner of his eye, notices this and deliberately interferes with the catcher's throw to second base. Nevertheless, the catcher throws out the runner at second. In the meantime, the runner from second rounds third too far and is thrown out by the second baseman while trying to return to the base.

Is the whole play called back?

*   *   *

No. If there had been any advance on the bases, the batter would have been called out for interference. But since a runner attempting to advance is put out, he and not the batter is called out. Other runners may advance at their own risk, too. If a runner is retired, there is no interference called. Rule 6.06 (c).

*   *   *

In Game Three of the 1975 World Series, a controversial play figured in the scoring of the winning run. In the bottom of the tenth inning, the Reds had Cesar Geronimo on first base with no out and Ed Armbrister at the plate. Armbrister laid down a bunt that bounced high in front of the plate, but the batter made no attempt to run. Red Sox catcher Carlton Fisk got tangled up with Armbrister after he had fielded the ball, and his subsequent throw to second base to force Geronimo sailed into center field. Geronimo continued to third on the play with Armbrister reaching first after a late start. The Reds went on to win the game, 6-5.

Plate umpire Larry Barnett didn't call offensive interference against Armbrister. If he had, the Red Sox would have had the right to elect the penalty rather than the play. Armbrister would have been called out, and Geronimo would have been returned to first base. Rule 6.06 (c).

Unaware

In a real game, in August 1979, the Reds were leading the host Pirates in the bottom of the fourth inning. But the Pirates got runners on first and third with two out. Fred Norman had a three-two count on batter Omar Moreno. On the pay-off pitch Lee Lacy at first was off-and-running from first base. Catcher Johnny Bench instinctively threw the ball to shortstop Davey Concepcion, who applied the tag to the sliding Lacy. The umpire called Lacy out.

Lacy, thinking his side was out, then got up and walked towards the first-base line, waiting to be delivered his glove for the field. Lacy was unaware that the pitch to Moreno had been wide and high for ball four. He had been forced to advance on the walk.

When his teammates yelled that fact to him, and that he should return to second, Concepcion was waiting for him at the bag with the ball. The umpire called Lacy out for the second time.

Pirate manager Chuck Tanner argued the call for a long time. Did his argument prevail?

* * *

No. When it didn't, he protested the game. But National League President Chub Feeney overruled it on two grounds: one, there had been no misinterpretation of rules, and two, Lacy should have known what was going on.

"Who says I can't run the bases in reverse when I hit a home run?"

The "Wild Hoss"

They didn't call John Leonard Roosevelt "Pepper" Martin the "Wild Hoss of the Osage" for nothing. Martin used to run wild on the bases.

In the 1931 and 1934 World Series, for example, Martin stole five and two bases, respectively—all of them, by the way, off Hall-of-Fame catcher Mickey Cochrane. His team, the Cardinals, won the the World Series both of those years.

Martin liked to "cut the pie," that is, show off from time to time. His big moment came during the 1933 season when "Pepper" hit a home run over the fence, and proceeded to run the bases in reverse order!

Is that legal?

* * *

No, it isn't. Up until 1921 it was, though. After the 1920 season the rule book was amended to read, "Running the bases in reverse order for the purpose either of confusing the fielders or making a travesty of the game is prohibited." Rule. 7.02 and 7.10 (b). When he reached home plate, Martin was called out.

* * *

Thirty years later, in 1963, another zany player, Jimmy Piersall, who was winding down his career with the equally zany Mets of that era, hit his 100th career home run one day, and he decided to celebrate the event in memorable fashion: he ran the bases in reverse order. But he was not called out. The play hadn't happened in such a long time that the umpires had forgotten about the rule. But Piersall's circuitous route that day brought so much media attention to the rule that no player in the last thirty years has attempted to follow in his footsteps.

The Trap

In a game between the visiting Cubs and the Los Angeles Dodgers, manager Tommy LaSorda's charges have runners on first and second base with one out in the bottom of the sixth inning. Then Darryl Strawberry hits a towering pop fly to very short right field. Andre Dawson calls second baseman Ryne Sandberg off the play and proceeds to deliberately let the ball drop. But he recovers and throws the ball to shortstop Jose Vizcaino for a play on Brett Butler at second base, and Vizcaino proceeds to run down and tag out the other Dodger runner for an inning-ending double play.

Is this a legitimate play?

* * *

No, but it used to be, until the Infield Fly Rule was imposed. Before that, right fielder Tommy Henrich and second baseman Joe Gordon of the Yankees in the mid-1940s perfected this ruse against the opposition. Henrich would call Gordon off the ball and drop the ball, hoping that the umpires would waive off the infield fly rule because this was an outfield fly. Henrich would then pursue his best option. Sometimes he would get a double play via the above example. If the batter didn't run out the play, he would initiate either a right-fielder-to-shortstop-to-first-baseman double play, or a right-fielder-to-second-baseman (force out) or -to-first-baseman (tag-out) double play. Occasionally, he would settle for a force out on a speedier runner at an advance base.

American League President William Harridge amended the rule because of Henrich's subterfuge. Now Rule 6.05 (1) reads, "If an infielder (or outfielder) intentionally drops a fair fly ball or line drive, with first, first and second, first and third, or first, second, and third base occupied before two are out, the ball is dead and the runner or runners shall return to their original base or bases."

The amendment didn't stop Henrich's craftiness, though. He simply mastered the art of trapping the ball, continuing to execute all of the above options.

Today, in this situation, the batter is not out if the infielder (or outfielder) permits the ball to drop untouched to the ground, except when the Infield Fly Rule applies. Rule 6.05 (1) APPROVED RULING.

Lines Are Lines

David Cone is the pitcher for the Mets. Mackey Sasser is the catcher. Cone blows the batter away with a swinging strike on a hard slider that goes down and away, but Sasser has trouble holding onto the pitch and it bounces about five feet to his right.

Since there is no one on base and no out, the batter runs out the play, but in running the last half of the distance from home to first, he runs "outside" of the three-foot line, and Sasser's throw to first baseman Eddie Murray hits him and bounces down the right-field line. The batter goes to second base on the play.

Does he have to give up his base?

* * *

Yes, he is called out because he has interfered with Sasser's throw. The only time a batter can run inside or outside the three-foot line is when he is trying to avoid a fielder trying to play a batted ball. Rule 6.05 (k).

A few years back, that same play occurred in a Mariner-Yankee game at Yankee Stadium. Don Slaught was the Yank catcher, Don Mattingly the first baseman. The Seattle batter-runner was called out for interference.

To Retouch or Not

This play happened in a Pirates-Braves game. With Dick Groat of the Pirates on second base, Roberto Clemente hit a wicked line drive foul down the right-field line. Groat didn't bother to retouch second after the foul, which went uncaught.

The big-name pitcher for the Milwaukee Braves went to the set position on the mound and then wheeled and fired a "pick-off throw" to second. Only it went into center field. Groat advanced to third on the errant throw. Then the Brave pitcher took the set position, again threw to second base, and appealed Groat's failure to retouch second base after Clemente's foul.

Did the appeal work?

*   *   *

No. If the ball is dead because of an uncaught foul, it is not necessary for a returning runner to retouch intervening bases. Groat picks up a base on the play. Rule 7.08 (d).

Two for the Price of One

John Kruk of the Phillies hits what appears to be a certain double-play ball to Jose Lind, the Pirates' second baseman. Lind fields the ball cleanly and gives a perfect toss to shortstop Jay Bell, who has enough time to take two full steps to touch second on the right-field side of the base. But before Bell can relay the ball to first for the inning-ending double play, the baserunner from first veers deliberately out of his path to take out Bell, preventing him from making the throw.

What's the umpire's call, if any?

* * *

The umpire calls the batter out because of the runner's interference. Rule 6.05 (m).

* * *

This play has happened thousands of times in the major leagues. Today the umpires are more likely to penalize the flagrant runner. At one time it was merely considered part of the game.

In 1949, for example, the Yankees thought that the Red Sox were roughing up their shortstop, Phil Rizzuto. One day, in retaliation, Joe DiMaggio slid directly at Red Sox shortstop Vern Stephens, who was well out of the base path, to break up a double play. Stephens made no throw to first and the umpire assessed no penalty against DiMaggio and the batter-runner.

DiMaggio's slide had a twofold result: the runner was safe at first and the Red Sox left Rizzuto alone from that day forward.

But today it's different.

Ball Hits Helmet

Ivan Calderon, Spike Owen, and Tim Wallach are on third, second, and first bases, respectively, when Gary Carter hits a tailor-made double-play ball to the second baseman. But Wallach, in running from first to second, accidentally loses his batting helmet; the ball hits it and then bounces past the fielder into the outfield while two runs score and Tim advances to third base on the play.

Legal play?

* * *

Yes. In cases where a batting helmet is accidentally hit by a batted or thrown ball, the ball remains in play. It is the same as if the helmet were not hit by the ball. Rule 6.05 (h).

* * *

Willie Mays, of course, was known for losing his hat while running the bases. Later, it became mandatory for players, beginning with the 1972 season, to wear a protective batting helmet. While with the Mets, in 1973, in Mays's last major-league season, he lost his helmet in the above situation while running between first and second base. Instead of a double play ensuing, the batter got credited with two runs batted in.

"The ball is still in play when it hits a helmet by accident."

Hoak Pulls a Hoax

Jackie Robinson of the 1947–56 Brooklyn Dodgers was responsible for the "Jackie Robinson Rule" being added to the rule book in 1956.

If Robinson was on second base, and another Brooklyn Dodger was on first base with less than two out, Robinson would deliberately let himself get hit during a tailor-made double play when the ball was hit his way. There was no rule to cover Robinson's "evasive" action at the time.

But then when Don Hoak of the 1954–55 Dodgers tried to mimic Robinson's move, the rulesmakers decided that the loophole had to be closed.

In a game between the Dodgers and the Milwaukee Braves in the middle of the 1955 campaign, Brooklyn had Hoak on second base and Duke Snider on first when Gil Hodges ripped a ground ball right at shortstop Johnny Logan. Hoak, realizing that this was certain to lead to an inning-ending double play, deliberately stuck out his foot and let the ball hit it. He was called out for runner's interference, but Snider was permitted to advance to second and Hodges, who was credited with a base hit, to first. The inning was still alive.

*   *   *

In 1956, this rule was amended. If that play were to occur today, both Hoak and Hodges would be called out. Rule 7.08 (b).

Catcher's Interference?

Suppose the visiting Red Sox and the Yankees, who are winning, 3-2, are hooked up in an important game in 1978. The Red Sox have Carlton Fisk on third base with one out in the top of the ninth inning. Dwight Evans then hits a vicious one-hopper right back at pitcher Ron Guidry, who wheels and fires to third baseman Craig Nettles, catching Fisk off base.

Fisk knows that his only chance to avoid the game's final out is to make a bold dash toward the plate, as though he's going to beat Nettles' throw to catcher Thurman Munson. But Munson, sensing that Fisk is going to be safe, moves up the third-base line, and without the ball in his possession, decks Fisk with a shoulder block. Then he takes Nettles' throw and applies the tag to the stunned Red Sox catcher.

Fisk and Red Sox manager Don Zimmer jump all over the home plate umpire, demanding that catcher's interference be called. Do they get it?

* * *

Yes. The catcher, without the ball in his possession, can't block the baseline, and he certainly can't physically assault the runner. Fisk scores, Evans is placed at second base, and the 3-3 game continues.

* * *

In a critical September 27, 1928, game between the visiting Cubs and the New York Giants, a catcher's apparent interference and assault of a runner were ignored by veteran umpire Bill Klem. Manager John McGraw of the Giants contended for the rest of his life that that call cost his team the pennant.

Here's what happened: With one out in the bottom of the sixth inning, in the first game of a doubleheader, the Cubs were leading the Giants, 3-2. But New York had runners on second and third when Shanty Hogan hit the ball back at Cub pitcher Art Nehf, who turned and fired to third. Andy Reese reached the plate, but Cub catcher Gabby Hartnett hit him with a shoulder block and knocked him down. Then the Bruin backstop threw his arms around Reese and held him until the third baseman tagged the runner out.

McGraw screamed for interference but Klem wouldn't grant it. The Giants played the game under protest, but the league office upheld Klem's decision.

The game was played long before the days of instant replay. But pictures in the papers the following day clearly indicted both Hartnett's actions and Klem's lack of same.

The Karate Chop

Back in the days when Randy Hundley was the catcher of the Cubs, Gene Mauch was the manager of the Expos, and there was no specific rule that covered a backstop's right to enter a dugout to catch a pop fly. Hundley entered the Montreal dugout one day to make what appeared to be a legal catch, when Mauch hit the Bruin backstop with a karate chop, causing the catcher to drop the ball.

Was Mauch's act a legal one?

* * *

Yes, at the time, it was. It was considered to be no different than an outfielder reaching into the stands to catch a ball and being hit with a karate chop by an overzealous fan. Both acts would definitely be placed under the category of unethical and unsportsmanlike conduct, but at the same time they would also be classified as legal plays.

Today, a fielder or catcher may reach or step into, or go into, the dugout with one or both feet to make a catch, and if he holds the ball, the catch shall be allowed. The ball is in play. Rule 7.04 (c).

The Booted Play

The San Francisco Giants have Willie McGee on second base, Will Clark on first base, and Matt Williams at the plate, while the host Cubs have Dave Smith on in relief. Smith's first pitch to Williams bounces in front of the plate and off the Bruin backstop's shinguard towards the first-base dugout. McGee and Clark move up a base on the wild pitch. But the Cub catcher, in running down the ball, accidentally kicks it into the Cubs' dugout.

What's the ruling? Is it true that runners can advance only one base on a wild pitch?

*   *   *

Yes, runners may advance only one base on a wild pitch that goes into dead territory. However, if the wild-pitch ball remains on the playing field, and is *subsequently* kicked or deflected into dead territory, the runners shall be awarded two bases from the position the runners are in at the time of the pitch. Rule 7.05 (h) APPROVED RULING. McGee scores and Clark advances to third.

*   *   *

Early in the 1992 season, a Yankee catcher inadvertently made the above *faux pas*.

Team Pranksters

Has it always been the custom for defensive players to carry their gloves with them to and from the bench?

*   *   *

No. Players used to leave their gloves on the field, out of the way of the opposing team. It wasn't until 1954 that the defensive players were required to carry their gloves to their dugout.

Phil Rizzuto began doing it earlier, around 1949, for his own reasons. Frank Shea, the former pitcher with the Yankees, has some theories behind Rizzuto's "reasons":

"When we used to have a home game on a Sunday and the following day off, I used to go home to Naugatuck, Connecticut, and look for garden snakes and worms. I'd come back the next night and give them to Johnny Lindell, who used to put them in Phil's glove on the field. In those days the fielders used to leave their gloves on the field. Lindell would come in from left field, drop his glove, pick up Phil's, and put the worms in it. Phil would go out to the field for the next inning, put his glove on, and then raise hell, saying he wouldn't play unless he had a different glove. And he meant it. He was afraid of almost everything."

"Those boys are up to some shenanigans, I have a feeling."

Firm Control of Body

The Dodgers have Brett Butler, the potential winning run on third base with one out when Juan Samuel lifts a high pop foul towards the San Diego dugout. Padre catcher Benito Santiago drifts towards the dugout, and when he sees that the ball is fading farther from him than he thought, he steps into the dugout to make the catch.

Should he have permitted the ball to fall to the ground untouched?

* * *

No. Santiago made a good play. He can make a legal throw from the dugout or he can step out of the dugout and make a play.

* * *

Suppose that after he had made the catch he slipped and fell to the dugout floor?

* * *

That would have been a bad play. The player has to maintain firm control of his body in order to make a follow-up play. If he loses control of his body, the ball becomes dead and all runners advance one base. Butler would score and the Dodgers would win the game. Rule 7.04 (c).

* * *

In 1947 big Ernie Lombardi was winding down his Hall-of-Fame career with the New York Giants. One day at the Polo Grounds, in a game with the Giants, St. Louis had Enos Slaughter on third base when Al Schoendienst lifted a foul pop towards the Redbirds' bench. Lombardi went into the dugout to make the catch, but he subsequently slipped and fell, and Slaughter was waved home by the plate umpire.

"The Reading Rifle"

They used to call outfielder Carl Furillo of the Brooklyn Dodgers "The Reading Rifle" because of his strong throwing arm. The short right-field wall at Ebbets Field helped him, also. Many times on a solid "hit" to right field Furillo threw the batter-runner out at first base.

One day the visiting New York Giants had Eddie Stanky on first base and Alvin Dark at the plate. With Stanky running on the pitch, Dark lined a one-hop shot to Furillo, who, in trying to throw out the batter at first base, heaved the ball into the Dodger dugout. At the time Furillo released the ball, Stanky was one step beyond second base, and Dark was two steps shy of first.

Where did they end up on the play?

* * *

Stanky scored and Dark advanced to second base. Rule 7.05 (g). Runners advance two bases with ball in dugout.

Distracting the Batter

With Wade Boggs of the Red Sox at the plate, the Twin second baseman positions himself directly behind second and jumps up and down, waving his arms, in an attempt to distract the Boston third baseman's focus.

Is this legal?

*   *   *

No, but it used to be, before Eddie Stanky of the New York Giants brought undue attention to the play in the early 1950s. Today the umpire would stop play and warn the violator, telling him that if he continued to try to distract the batter, he would be ejected from the game.

*   *   *

The Twin mid-infielders actually tried a similar-type scam on Boggs, when he was on a torrid hitting streak in the mid-1980s. Second baseman Phil Lombardozzi and shortstop Phil Gagne changed positions just as the pitcher delivered the ball to the plate. Umpire Ed Brinkman stopped play and applied rule 4.06 (b). ILLEGAL DISTRACTION.

On the next pitch Boggs hit a line-drive double.

Run Ragged

Let's take some baseball license with the Brewers 22–2 rout of the Blue Jays in 1992. The Toronto center fielder, for the sake of deliberation, had a very rough day. He spent the entire game running down balls that had gotten in the gap. Finally, in a fit of exasperation, he threw his glove at a ball that was rolling to the right-center field wall, but he missed.

Is there any penalty?

*   *   *

No. If the glove had stopped the roll of the ball, each runner, including the batter-runner, may, without liability of being put out, advance three bases. Rule 7.05 (c).

* * *

When Hack Wilson was playing out the string for a bad Phillie club in 1934, he was fat and out of shape. (Wilson played his last seven major-league games with the Phillies.) One day, while Wilson was playing right field, the opposition was tattooing the right-field wall at Baker Bowl. By the eighth inning Wilson was huffing and puffing. Finally, he had had enough. When another long fly ball hit well up on the wall, bounced off it, and began to roll back towards the infield, Wilson threw his glove at the ball—but he missed it.

The Phillie second baseman later snickered to the shortstop, "It doesn't surprise me. He can't hit the cut-off man, either."

They Won but They Lost

In a late-season game in 1979, Yankee first baseman Chris Chambliss was warming up his infielders in between innings when the webbing of his glove broke. While he ran to the dugout to get a new glove, Lou Piniella came out to first to continue the warm-ups. When Chambliss resumed his first-base position, Tiger manager Sparky Anderson came out to the plate umpire and said that once a substitute took the place of a player on the field, he was in the game. When the umpire didn't remove Chambliss from the game, Anderson filed a protest. The Yankees went on to win the game, 3-1.

Did Anderson win the protest?

* * *

Yes, he did, but the league office considered it a technicality and elected not to play the game over. Sparky won but he lost.

"Sorry, folks, but I've got to catch this."

A Matter of Judgment

In a game at the Oakland Coliseum, Kelly Gruber of the Blue Jays hits a soft pop foul towards the third-box seats. The A's third baseman, Carney Lansford, makes a running catch about 10 feet from the boxes, but his momentum carries him into the wire protecting fence, the ball dropping out of his glove upon contact.

Is it a legal catch?

* * *

It's a matter of judgment on the umpire's part. The rule book says that if the fielder has contact with another fielder or wall immediately following his contact with the ball—and drops it—it is not a legal catch. Ten feet would seem to be a considerable distance, but it wasn't in the following application. Rule 2.00 CATCH.

* * *

Late in the 1982 season, the host Braves were leading the Padres when San Diego's Gene Richards, with no one on and two out, sent a twisting fly ball down the left-field line. Terry Harper made a running catch inside the foul line, but his momentum carried him across the line into the bullpen railing. Trying to cushion his landing, he grabbed the railing but dropped the ball. Umpire Ed Vargo called the play a no-catch, and by the time Harper retrieved the ball and returned it to the infield, Richards had circled the bases. The official scorer ruled the play a four-base error, but the league office overruled the scoring and called the play an inside-the-park home run.

Wild Abandonment

In a game between the visiting Mets and the Pirates, New York has two out and a one-two count on their pitcher at the plate. The batter swings and misses the next offering by the Buc moundsman. It's a strikeout, but the Buc backstop deliberately drops the ball. It is a hot and humid day, and he wants to tire the Met pitcher by forcing him to run to first base. Instead, the pitcher walks back to his team's dugout. When he gets to the lip of the dugout, the Pirate catcher in resignation tosses the ball back to the mound and heads for his own dugout.

Good play?

* * *

No. The batter may advance to first base at any time before he enters the dugout. Rule 7.08 (a) APPROVED RULING. In this case it didn't matter, but in a 1947 game it did.

In a 1947 game at Yankee Stadium, the visiting catcher tried to get Bobo Newsom to run in a similar-type situation with only one out. Before the pitcher threw the first pitch to the following batter, Newsom, who had entered the dugout, sneaked to the far side, crept up the steps, and made a mad dash to first. The pitcher, watching, waited until Bobo had expended his maximum amount of energy and then fired to the first baseman for the out. A runner could do that then. Today Newsom would be called out as soon as he entered the dugout.

Medwick Was Ducking

Can a player be removed from a game for his own protection?

*   *   *

According to past practice, he can. In the top of the sixth inning, in the final game of the 1934 World Series, Joe "Ducky" Medwick slid hard into Tiger third baseman Marv Owen. The collision led to a confrontation between the two players. At the time, the Cardinals were leading the host Tigers, so the Detroit crowd was in a hostile mood.

When Medwick went out to his position in left field in the bottom half of the inning, the Tiger fans bombarded Medwick with bottles, fruit, vegetables, and tennis balls. When it became obvious that the belligerent crowd didn't intend to let up its cascade of objects on the unrecalcitrant Redbird, Commissioner Judge Kenesaw Mountain Landis, who was in attendance, instructed the umpires to remove Medwick from the game, partly for the player's safety and partly for the game's protection.

The Cardinals went on to win the game, 11-0, and the world championship.

The Oriole Rule

Do all fielders' gloves have to meet certain specifications?

*   *   *

They do now, but that wasn't always the case. Until the early 1960s the catcher was allowed to wear a leather glove or mitt of any size, shape, or weight.

Towards the end of the 1958 season, the Orioles purchased Hoyt Wilhelm from the Indians. Wilhelm, who went on to win 143 games and save 227 contests in his career, was a great knuckleball pitcher. But his Baltimore catcher, Gus Triandos, had special difficulty following the dance patterns of Wilhelm's knuckler. Triandos was a good long-ball hitter—167 career homers—but only an average defensive player. When Wilhelm was pitching, he was a less-than-average defensive catcher. He spent most of his time behind the plate running back to the screen to retrieve passed balls.

So Oriole manager Paul Richards came up with a solution to the problem. When Wilhelm would pitch, Triandos would wear an oversized mitt. It had a circumference of 45 inches. Overall, the oversized mitt helped Triandos. But it didn't help later Oriole catchers. Back-up catcher Charlie Lau of the 1961 Orioles had five passed balls in one game, three of them coming in the same inning.

Visiting teams complained so much about the oversized Oriole glove, however, that in 1965 the rule was amended to prohibit gloves with a circumference of more than 38 inches. Rule 1.12: the so-called "Oriole Rule."

A Vacant Rule

In this hypothetical case, with two out in the bottom of the ninth inning, the home team Phillies are trailing the Pirates, 7-6. John Kruk is the Philadelphia batter, and Lenny Dykstra the runner at first base.

On the first pitch, from Pittsburgh hurler Doug Drabek, Kruk lifts a high pop foul towards the Phillie dugout. As Pirate first baseman Orlando Merced and catcher Don Slaught converge on the ball, the on-deck batter, Darren Daulton, gets caught in the crossfire. Merced runs into Daulton and drops the ball. The Pirates demand of the home-plate umpire that Kruk be called out because of offensive interference.

Does the umpire comply with the Pittsburgh request?

* * *

According to the language of Rule 7.11, he should, but he probably doesn't. The rule says, "The players, coaches or any member of an offensive team shall vacate any space (including both dugouts) needed by a fielder who is attempting to field a batted or thrown ball. PENALTY: Interference shall be called and the batter or runner on whom the play is being made shall be declared out."

But quite often the umpires don't interpret Rule 7.11 literally. If they feel that the on-deck batter made a legitimate attempt to get out of the way of the ball, they probably don't call offensive interference. In the above example, Kruk would probably get at least one more swing at a pitch.

* * *

At least that's the way the rule was interpreted in a game between the Oakland A's and the Orioles in a 1976 game.

Sal Bando was the Oakland batter and Larry Haney the on-deck hitter. The Orioles' third baseman and catcher attempted to make the play, Haney tried to get out of their way, and the ball fell untouched to the ground. Baltimore wanted an interference call, but the umpire behind the plate wouldn't give it. Play continued. Bando tripled and eventually scored the winning run.

In essence, the umpires don't interpret Rule 7.11 as rigidly as it's stated.

Indecisive Runner

The Brewers have a runner on first base when the batter bunts a ball towards Royal first baseman Wally Joyner. Noticing that the Milwaukee batter is not running out the play, Joyner allows the ball to bounce, picks it up, steps on first, and tags the runner who is trying to return to first.

Good play?

* * *

Excellent. A legal double play. Rule 6.05 (l) APPROVED RULING.

* * *

In 1949, Yankee first baseman Tommy Henrich, who was a "heads-up player," fielded such a bunt by Washington Senator outfielder Buddy Stewart with Eddie Yost on first base. "Old Reliable" turned the one-hop bunt into a double play.

A Little Sand in Your Shoes

Bip Roberts of the Reds is the batter with the bases loaded, two out, and a three-two count, when the opposing catcher throws sand on his shoes just after the pitcher has released the ball. Roberts, who is distracted, swings and misses for the third out. Of course, he argues vehemently with the plate umpire before he accepts the verdict.

Is the umpire supportive?

*   *   *

Probably not. He probably didn't see the violation.

*   *   *

Should he have asked the other umpires?

*   *   *

According to the rule book, yes. In this example, Roberts should have been awarded first base on catcher's interference, and each runner should have advanced one base. Rule 7.04 (d).

*   *   *

Birdie Tebbets of the Red Sox in the late 1940s liked to use this form of distraction. Usually he got away with it. But one day the plate umpire was alert. He looked out at the second-base umpire, who flashed him the violation sign, and the plate umpire awarded the batter first base. Tebbetts didn't argue long. He knew the plate umpire hadn't seen his ruse, but he didn't want to draw attention to it.

Fan Interference?

In the top of the eighth inning of a hypothetical game, between the visiting White Sox and the Yankees, Frank Thomas pulls a ball into the right-field corner with one out. Right fielder Danny Tartabull moves to play the carom of the ball off the wall, but when he sees a fan reach over the wall and "appear to touch it" as he tumbles out of the stands onto the playing field, he backs off, thinking that the fan's interference had created a ground-rule double. Finally, Tartabull picks up the ball and returns it to the infield, but not before Thomas has raced all the way to third base. Tartabull and the Yankees argue that Thomas should be forced to return to second base because of the fan's interference.

Is that the way the first-base umpire sees the play?

* * *

Not necessarily. In a similar real-life game on July 4, 1986, John Cangelosi of the White Sox was the batter—at Comiskey Park—and Claudell Washington was the Yankee right fielder who took his time fielding the ball because he anticipated the interference call. But first-base umpire Mike Reilly said that when a fan touches the ball, it usually changes direction, and this one, in his opinion, never did. He also said that a fan's falling on the field is not interference unless it impedes the play.

The play stood. Ozzie Guillen then hit a sacrifice fly that proved to be the difference in Chicago's 2–1 victory over New York.

The Batting Helmet Flap

Do all present-day major league players have to wear an ear flap on their protective batting helmets?

* * *

No, they don't. But, every player who has come into the major leagues since the 1983 season must wear a single ear-flap helmet though the same players may opt to wear a double ear-flap helmet. Any players who were in the majors in 1982 and recorded at that time their objection to wearing a single ear-flap helmet don't have to don one.

It's amazing that anyone who was playing in the major leagues in 1982 would object to wearing an ear flap after seeing Ron Cey of the 1981 Los Angeles Dodgers beaned by a Rich "Goose" Gossage fastball in that year's World Series. If he hadn't been wearing a protective helmet, he would have been seriously injured, perhaps as seriously as Mickey Cochrane, whose career came to an end after being hit with a Bump Hadley beanball in 1937, and Joe Medwick, whose career was never the same after Bob Bowman of the Cardinals felled him in 1940.

By the way, protective helmets were first worn by some members of the Brooklyn Dodgers in 1941, after two sensational rookies, Pete Reiser and Pee Wee Reese, were hospitalized for substantial stays after serious beanings.

The protective helmet was made mandatory in 1971.

"With these carpet-covered concrete fields, there's no telling where the ball will bounce."

Pantomime Show

Let us say it is "Old-Uniform Day" at Riverfront Stadium, and some of the Red players are wearing the baggy uniforms of the 1940s. (The Reds had such a day at the end of August during the 1992 season.)

Tony Gwynn of the Padres is on third base with one out when Fred McGriff hits a turf-cutter to shortstop Barry Larkin, who is playing up on the Astroturf line that delineates the boundaries of the inner portion of the infield. Gwynn holds at third. But instead of throwing the ball to first for the out, Larkin begins to wiggle his arms and pat his uniform with his hand and glove. Gwynn thinks that Larkin is decoying him, so he remains fixed at third. But in reality the ball has rolled up Larkin's sleeve and down his shirt.

How does the umpire unravel this one?

* * *

When the ball becomes part of a defensive man's uniform, each runner is allowed to advance one base without liability of being put out. Even though Gwynn didn't try to advance, he is entitled to one base. Rule 9.01 (c).

* * *

This play occurred in a 1948 game between the Philadelphia Athletics and the Red Sox. With Ted Williams on third base, the ball rolled up shortstop Eddie Joost's sleeve and inside his shirt. Williams thought that Joost was conning him, but after the play he got a one-base advance.

Seven Men on the Field

Suppose that in a game between the Tigers and the host Indians, a ball from the bullpen in left field ends up on the playing field. The Cleveland left fielder retrieves it and runs it over to the Bengals' substitute catcher in foul territory, and hands it to him. While the left fielder is in foul territory, the Cleveland pitcher delivers the ball to the plate.

Does the third-base umpire call time out, or does he assess a penalty on the play?

* * *

He calls a balk. If any defensive player is in foul territory, the penalty is a balk. Rule 4.03.

* * *

In an early season game in 1984, Red Sox second baseman Jerry Remy ran into foul territory to track down his errant throw to first base in between innings. While he was doing so, Bruce Hurst delivered an official pitch to the first batter of the new inning. But the home plate umpire correctly called a balk against Hurst and declared the offering a no-pitch.

☻ 2 ☻

UNUSUAL SITUATIONS

Balk Talk

With Paul Molitor of the Brewers at first base, the Tiger pitcher, in the set-position stance with the ball in his glove and his pitching arm at his side, takes his sign, removes the ball from his glove, and moves to the set position.
Good move?

*   *   *

No, it's a balk.

*   *   *

Suppose instead of doing the above, the pitcher receives the ball from his catcher and with his feet in the set-position stance nervously bounces the ball in his glove a few times or removes the ball from his glove.
Balk?

*   *   *

Yes. In both cases. The limitations on a pitcher's movements start when he intentionally contacts the rubber with his pivot foot. Rule 8.01 (a) and (b).

In Front of the Runner

Let's go one step further with the preceding situations. Molitor is now at second base. The Tiger pitcher, anticipating that Molitor is going to attempt to steal third, takes his stretch and comes to a stop. Then, as the Brewer infielder breaks for the advance bag, he throws to third baseman Tony Phillips for the "out." Is Molitor out?

*   *   *

Yes, provided the Tiger moundsman did not start a pitch after his stretch-and-stop.

*   *   *

Suppose Molitor had not been running on the play?

*   *   *

The pitcher can't throw to an unoccupied base. If he does, it is a balk. Rule 8.05 (d).

Double Violation

Greg Maddux is the pitcher for the Cubs, and Marquis Grissom, who represents the lead run for the Expos, is on third base. The batter's focus is on the third-base coach. The batter doesn't want to miss a sign in this key situation. Maddux comes to the set position and stares at Grissom, who is trying to get a long lead at third. Just as Maddux moves into his delivery and picks up the catcher's target, he notices that the batter has stepped out of the box, and he stops his movement towards the plate.

What's the umpire's call?

*   *   *

It is a double violation. The umpire will not call a balk. He will call time, and both the batter and pitcher will start over from "scratch." Rule 6.02 (b).

A Clean Play

The Atlanta Brave starter digs himself into a hole in the top of the sixth inning when he walks three consecutive batters with two out.

Then, with Howard Johnson of the Mets standing at the plate, the Brave hurler goes to his "ace in the hole"—a spitter. As soon as he throws it, the home-plate umpire calls, "Ball four," but Johnson swings at the pitch and hits it over the right-field wall for a grand-slam home run.

Manager Jeff Torborg of the Mets immediately runs out to home plate and tells the umpire that he elects to take the play over the penalty.

Can he do this?

* * *

Yes, he can. The umpire allows the play. Rule 8.02 (a) PENALTY and 8.02 (c). The umpire still warns the pitcher, however, against throwing a spitball. If he repeats the violation, he is subject to a fine by the league office.

The *Faux Pas*

Delino DeShields is on first base for the Expos with Larry Walker at the plate. The Chicago Cub pitcher, in the set position, quickly steps off the rubber with his pivot foot and fires the ball towards the plate. Walker hits the ball over the wall at Wrigley Field for an apparent two-run homer.

Do the runs count?

* * *

No. The pitcher's action was a balk. Rule 8.05 (e). Once he disengaged his foot from the rubber, he became an infielder. A batter can't hit an infielder's throw. If the batter had hit the offering by the pitcher while he had his pivot foot on the rubber, the Expos could have elected to take the two-run homer in place of the balk. But in the above example, it is a balk. DeShields would advance to second base, and the count on Walker would remain the same.

The Spitball Rule

The Mets have the bases loaded in a game against the visiting Astros. Eddie Murray is the batter with a three-two count in a 3–3 game. Before the Astro reliever delivers the pay-off pitch, on this balmy night, he reaches the ball up to his mouth and blows on it, and then he fires a pitch that Murray swings through for strike three.

The game goes to extra innings. Or does it?

* * *

No. The game ends right there. As soon as the pitcher brought the ball to his mouth, the umpire calls a ball on the pitcher. Murray walks and the winning run is forced home.

The pitcher may not bring the ball to his mouth, except when the weather is cold and both managers, before the game, agree to waive the rule. The first time the pitcher does it, the umpire may award a ball to the batter. The second time he does it, he may eject the pitcher from the game. Rule 8.02 (a).

The Good-Hitting Pitcher

One day in 1977 Ken Brett of the White Sox was the starting pitcher, and Brian Downing the designated hitter. Brett pitched well for seven innings, but in the eighth he ran into trouble. It was time for a change. White Sox manager Bob Lemon knew that. But he didn't want to remove Brett entirely from the game because Brett was a good hitter. In 1973 he had hit home runs in a record (for pitchers) four consecutive games. The opposing pitcher was an effective righthander. Downing was also a righthander. Lemon switched Brett to first base.

Does this affect the batting order?

* * *

Yes, it did affect things. Now he had 10 batters in the lineup. Once the game pitcher is switched from the mound to a defensive position, this move shall terminate the Designated Hitter role for the rest of the game. Rule 6.10 (b). Downing had to be taken out of the lineup. (The game pitcher may only *pinch-hit* for the D.H.)

The Quick Pick-off

Let us say that Devon White of the Blue Jays is on first base and Mike Flanagan is the pitcher for the Orioles. Flanagan stretches his arms and, without stopping, steps toward and throws to first baseman Glenn Davis, who slaps the tag on the sliding White.

Is Flanagan's move legal?

* * *

Yes. Stopping is necessary only before a pitch. Rule 8.01 (b).

Go Back Before You Go Forward

Rickey Henderson of the A's is on third base with one out in the sixth inning of a game against the host Indians. As the Cleveland pitcher goes into a slow wind-up, Henderson breaks for the plate. The Tribe hurler then steps forward off the mound and throws the ball to catcher Sandy Alomar for the "out" at the plate.

Does it count?

*   *   *

After assuming a wind-up position, the pitcher must step clearly backwards off the rubber with his pivot foot to change positions. The Indian pitcher's move is a balk. Henderson scores. Rule 8.01 (b).

Did He Swing?

Luis Polonia of the Angels starts to swing at White Sox relief pitcher Bobby Thigpen's forkball, but at the last second he tries to check his swing.

How does the umpire decide what to call the pitch?

*   *   *

The rule that most umpires use is as follows: If the bat is swung so that it is in front of the batter's body or ahead of it, it is a strike. Some umpires feel differently—that if the batter made an attempt to hit the ball, it is a strike.

The Good Bunter

Brett Butler of the Los Angeles Dodgers is a good bunter. During the 1991 season, for example, he had 21 bunt singles. Let us say that two of his bunts were the subjects of interesting umpire rule interpretations.

In the first situation, he bunted the ball down the first-base line, and then in releasing his bat, he accidentally let it hit the ball from behind so that it slithered in between the pitcher and the first baseman for a "base hit."

Does he get a base hit on that play?

* * *

No. When, after hitting or bunting a fair ball, his bat hits the ball a second time in fair territory, he is called out. The ball is dead and no runners may advance. Rule 6.05 (h).

On another occasion Butler bunted the ball down the first-base line, and just before the ball could roll foul, it rolled against the bat which he dropped in fair territory.

What's the umpire's call here?

* * *

If in the umpire's judgment, there was no intention to interfere with the course of the ball, the ball is alive and in play. Base hit for Butler. Rule 6.05 (h).

"Improper" Situations

Suppose the number-six man in the Atlanta Braves' batting order hits improperly in the number-five man's spot. He doubles in two runs. Then the "proper batter"—under the circumstances—completes his at-bat without an appeal from the defensive team.

Who is the "proper" batter to follow the "improper" one? Do the number-six man's double and two RBI count?

* * *

When an improper batter becomes a runner or is put out, and a pitch is made to the next batter before an appeal is made, the improper batter thereby becomes the proper batter, and the results of his time at-bat become legal. Rule 6.07 (c). In this instance, the number-six's at-bat became legal.

When the proper batter is called out because he has failed to bat in turn, the next batter shall be the batter whose name follows that of the proper batter thus called out. Rule 6.07 (d).

Putting a New Ball in Play

Andre Dawson of the Cubs is the batter for Chicago with two out and no one on base in the bottom of the eighth inning in a tie game. Steve Avery of the Braves pitches, Dawson swings and fouls the ball back to the brick backstop beneath the screen. When the ball bounces off the brick surface, all the way back to catcher Greg Olson, Dawson requests the plate umpire to put a new ball in play.

Does the umpire have to honor Dawson's request?

* * *

In this case he does, as the ball could have been scarred by hitting the wall. Some years back, the pitcher or batter could put in a request for a new ball on just about any whim he could invent. But today the ball has to hit a wall or get dirty in some way. And then the ball will be replaced only at the umpire's discretion.

In the above case, though, he would undoubtedly honor Dawson's request.

Reverse Form

In 1960, in a game between the Baltimore Orioles and the Chicago White Sox, the Birds were leading, 8–1, when Ted Kluszewski of the Palehose appeared to hit a three-run homer to close the score to 8–4. But just before the pitch, a ball from the bullpen had rolled out on the field, and the umpire had called, "Time." On the following pitch, Kluszewksi popped up to end the inning.

It appears that when a home run is negated by an umpire's call of timeout, the batter almost always seems to make an out on the next swing.

Are there any happy exceptions?

* * *

Yes. In the late 1940s, when the Brooklyn Dodgers and the Cardinals went down to the wire in just about every season, Stan Musial one day hit what appeared to be a grand slam. But, would you believe it (?), time had been called by an umpire. The "Man" went back to business as usual, and this time he hit a base-clearing triple.

Quick Exit?

Manager Sparky Anderson of the Tigers on this day selects a light-hitting batter as this designated hitter, and he puts him in the eighth spot in the batting order. But when his time at-bat comes in the second inning, the bases are loaded, and Sparky decides to go for the big inning. He sends up a long-ball hitter, Mickey Tettleton, for his DH.

Can he do this?

* * *

No, he can't. The designated hitter named in the starting lineup must come to bat at least one time, unless the opposing club changes pitchers. Rule 6.10 (b).

Fist Ball

The Twin batter has a count of two balls and two strikes when he swings and misses a Dave Stewart fastball. But the ball hits the batter's fist and bounces into foul territory down the first-base line. Catcher Terry Steinbach of the A's pounces on the ball and throws it to first baseman Mark McGwire, who steps on the base.

Do the A's have to make the above play?

* * *

No. The batter is out, and the ball becomes dead as soon as it hits the batter. In order for it to have been a foul ball, it would have had to hit the bat before it hit the batter. A batter is out when he attempts to hit a third strike and the ball touches him. Rule 6.05 (7).

The Unkindest Touch

The Mets have a runner on second base, one out, and Eddie Murray at the plate in a game against the host Phillies. Murray lofts a soft fly ball to left-center field. The runner, thinking that the ball might drop for a base hit, goes halfway to third, but the center fielder makes a good running catch.

His subsequent throw to third base, however, strikes a stone and bounces wildly past the third baseman into the Mets' dugout. The runner from second advances two bases on the play, scoring a run. *But* he doesn't retouch second before he makes his advance.

The Phillies realize this, so the pitcher, when he puts the ball in play, throws it first to second base and files an appeal with the umpire.

Is the run taken off the scoreboard?

*   *   *

Yes, the runner had to retouch second after the catch. Then, while the ball was dead, he could advance. The award of two bases would have been made from his original base. Rule 7.05 (i).

"Where did third base go to?"

The Base that Moved

With Mike Greenwell of the Red Sox on first base, in a game at Comiskey Park in Chicago, Wade Boggs hits a drive to left-center field that drops safely in the alley. Greenwell rounds second and heads towards third aiming to beat the center fielder's strong throw.

As Greenwell comes into third with a hard slide, he dislodges the base from its usual stationary spot and moves it a few feet into foul territory. At the same time, the throw hits Greenwell and bounds down the left-field line. Greenwell scores easily. But Boggs, who has taken second and now approaches third, doesn't know whether he should touch the base or the spot where it usually resides. He decides to touch the spot, and continue on to score, touching the plate, of course.

The White Sox appeal the play. Do they get an out?

*   *   *

No. The succeeding runner, on a play like that one, merely has to touch or occupy the point marked by the dislodged base. Rule 7.08 (c) APPROVED RULING (2).

Interfering with Catcher

Jose Guzman, pitching for the Rangers, has one out and a two-two count on the batter. The Mariners have Edgar Martinez on second base and Ken Griffey on first.

On Guzman's next pitch both runners break for their advance bases, the batter swings and misses, but interferes in the process with catcher Geno Petralli's attempt to throw out either runner.

The batter is already out. What penalty does the umpire assess against the Mariners?

* * *

The batter is out and the ball is dead. All runners must return to the last base that was, in the judgment of the umpire, legally touched at the time of the interference. Rule 6.06 (c).

Double Jeopardy

The Pirates have runners on second and third bases with one out. Jose Lind hits a come-backer to the Cardinal pitcher, and the runner at third gets caught in a rundown between third and home. During the rundown, the runner at second safely advances to third just before the trapped runner is called out for offensive interference.

Can the succeeding runner remain at third?

* * *

If, in a rundown between home and third base, the succeeding runner has advanced and is standing on third base when the runner in a rundown is called out *for offensive interference*, the umpire shall send the runner standing on third base back to second base. (The reasoning is that the runner shall advance on an interference play and a runner is considered to occupy a base until he legally has reached the next succeeding base.) Since the trapped runner had not legally reached home plate, he still occupied third base, negating the runner at second the legal right to advance to third. Rule 77.08 (6).

Interference Ignored

The Blue Jays have a runner on second base with two out and John Olerud at the plate. On the pitcher's next serve the catcher interferes with the batter's swing, but Olerud hits a ball anyway to the left of second base. The shortstop makes a long-reaching one-hand snag, but his off-balance throw takes the first baseman off the bag on the outfield side of the base, and Olerud is safe.

In the meantime, the runner at second rounds third and heads for the plate. The first baseman recovers, and throws to the catcher in time for the out.

Is that the third out of the inning, or does the offensive team, because of the catcher's interference, get to elect the penalty rather than the play?

* * *

The runner caught at the plate became the third out of the inning. Since the batter reached first base safely and the runner from second advanced at least one base, play proceeds without reference to the interference. Rule 6.08 (c).

Force Out?

With one out, the Cardinals have Felix Jose on third base, Todd Zeile on second base, and Ozzie Smith on first base. Pedro Guerrero then hits a ground ball to Met shortstop Dick Schofield, who throws to second baseman Willie Randolph for the start of a double play, but Smith beats the throw. Randolph, however, relays the ball to first baseman Eddie Murray for the out on Guerrero.

Murray notices that Smith has overslid second base, throws to Schofield, who applies the tag to the runner before he can scramble back to the base.

In the meantime, Jose and Zeile have scored on the play. However, the Mets argue that the runs shouldn't count, since the inning ended on a force-out double play.

Are they right?

* * *

No, they are not right. The runs score. It is not a force play. It is a tag play. Rule 7.08 (e) PLAY.

Comedy of Errors

Suppose the Montreal Expo batter hits a ground ball to the Chicago Cub shortstop and ends up on second base, when the Bruin infielder throws the ball into the first-base stands. However, the batter-runner missed touching first base. Even though he was "awarded" second base, and the ball is dead, can the defensive team throw to the untouched base for an appeal on him when the ball becomes live?

* * *

Yes. Rule 7.05 (i).

Infield Fly—If Fair

The Yankees have the bases loaded and no out, when Danny Tartabull hits a towering pop fly down the third-base line. The umpire immediately calls, "Infield fly, if fair." The Indian third baseman moves in to make the play, but the wind is playing havoc with the high pop.

In the meantime, the Cleveland pitcher runs to third to cover the open base. The third baseman staggers under the ball, which eventually lands untouched in foul territory, but bounces directly to the fielder in fair territory. The third baseman grabs the ball and immediately throws it to the pitcher, who is on the bag at third. The pitcher relays the ball to the second baseman, who throws it to the first baseman. None of the runners leave their bases on the play.

Triple play?

*　*　*

No. The only out the Indians get is the batter—on the infield fly rule. The ball is neither fair nor foul until it is touched. In this case it was touched in fair territory, so it is a fair ball. On an infield fly, which could be handled with ordinary effort, the runners advance only at their own risk. Rule 2.00 INFIELD FLY. See next page.

Learn the Tricky Infield Fly Rule

Once again the Yankees have runners on third, second, and first bases, respectively, when Don Mattingly hits a high pop fly towards the Indian first baseman. The umpire calls, "Infield fly, if fair." All of the runners stay close to their bases.

The first baseman, knowing the rule, lets the ball fall to the ground untouched. But he catches the ball on the first bounce and steps on first base. Indecisively, not conversant with the rule, the runner at first steps off the bag, and is tagged by the first baseman. In the meantime, the runner at third bolts for the plate and is thrown out by a throw from the first baseman to the catcher.

Triple play?

* * *

Yes. All the runners were mixed up. First of all, the first baseman didn't have to touch first. The batter was already out on the infield fly. But the first baseman's act of touching first base confused the runner on first into thinking that he was forced to advance on the play. The runner, of course, can advance at his own risk after the infield fly is caught or dropped, so he became the second out. The runner at third, also advancing at his own risk, became the third out of the inning. Rule 2.00 INFIELD FLY.

A Risky Play

A Cleveland runner is at second base when Brook Jacoby swings at a Tim Leary pitch and is obstructed by the Yankee catcher. But Jacoby still manages to line a single to left field. The runner at second didn't get a good jump on the play, because there was a chance that Yankee third baseman Charlie Hayes might snag the liner, but he attempts to score anyway. However, left fielder Roberto Kelly whips a strong throw to the plate and guns down the Indian runner.

Is the play called back because of the catcher's obstruction?

* * *

No. Since the batter-runner advanced at least one base, the obstruction is waived off. The other advanced past third at his own risk, and his out stands. Rule 6.08 (c).

Suicide Squeeze

In the bottom of the ninth inning, Shawon Dunston of the Cubs, who is at third base, represents the winning run. Mark Grace is the batter with one out.

Grace is interfered with by the catcher as he attempts a suicide squeeze bunt on the first pitch to him. Dunston, who is running on the pitch, is an easy out at the plate when the catcher picks up the ball in fair territory and applies the tag.

Does Grace get first base on the catcher's interference? Is Dunston out?

* * *

Grace is awarded first base and Dunston scores, if the Cub manager elects the penalty over the play. Whenever the catcher interferes with the batter, the offensive player is awarded first base. If, on such interference, a runner is attempting to score on a squeeze or steal from third, the ball is proclaimed dead and the runner on third scores.

Knockdown

Terry Pendleton of the Braves is on first base when David Justice lashes a single to right field. Pendleton rounds second widely and continues to third as the Cincinnati Red right fielder unleashes a wide throw to the outfield side of third base. Third baseman Chris Sabo, in trying to field the ball, runs into and knocks Pendleton to the ground in the process of catching the ball. Is defensive interference called? Does any defensive player receive an error? Where do Pendleton and Justice end up?

* * *

Yes. Sabo is charged with obstruction. (Rule 7.06a) He also picks up an error on the play. Pendleton and Justice are each awarded an advance base, Pendleton to score and Justice to second.

Clean Catch?

The Houston Astros have Jeff Bagwell on second base, Craig Biggio on first, and Ken Caminiti at the plate with a three-two count and two out. Caminiti swings and misses the pay-off pitch, which bounces off the catcher's glove and becomes pinned to the chest protector of the Brave backstop.

Can all the runners advance? Or is it a legal catch?

* * *

Caminiti is out on a strikeout and the Astros are retired on outs. Rule 6.05 (b). The catch is legal.

Two Trips Per Inning

Scott Erickson, the pitcher for the Twins, is in trouble in the bottom half of the sixth inning. The Brewers have Jim Gantner on third, Paul Molitor on second, and Robin Yount on first with one out. Before Erickson pitches to clean-up hitter Rob Deer, Minnesota manager Tom Kelly comes out to the mound, explaining to his righthander how he wants him to throw to Deer.

Erickson, perhaps thinking too hard, proceeds to walk Deer on four straight pitches. Kelly then comes out to the mound for the second time in the inning, and everyone in the ballpark knows what's going to happen.

What?

*   *   *

A second trip by the manager to the same pitcher in the same inning causes the hurler's automatic removal. Rule 8.06 (a).

One Trip Per Batter

Suppose in the preceding example, manager Tom Kelly had come out to the mound for the second time just after Erickson had thrown ball three to Deer.

*   *   *

The penalty would be greater. The manager or coach can't make a second trip to the mound while the same hitter is at the plate. Rule 8.06 (a). If the manager does, he is automatically ejected from the game, but the pitcher can remain for the duration of the hitter's at-bat. After the batter either reaches base or makes an out, the pitcher is ejected, too.

The Manager's Clone

Let's take the preceding situation one step further. Suppose Kelly has already made his one trip to the mound, but after Deer runs the count to three-oh, Kelly yells some instructions to shortstop Greg Gagne, who runs to the mound to converse with Erickson.

Is there any penalty?

* * *

Yes. Gagne's trip to the mound would be considered Minnesota's second conference during the same at-bat, and the same penalties that were imposed when Kelly visited the mound twice during the same hitter's at-bat would apply here. Rule 8.06 (a).

* * *

The rule wasn't always applied so rigidly. Casey Stengel frequently used to manage through his infielders, who didn't always relish the role of playing manager.

Once during the 1949 World Series, when Tommy "Wild Man" Byrne had walked the bases loaded against the Brooklyn Dodgers, Casey whistled to second baseman Jerry Coleman. That was his signal that he wanted Coleman to visit the mound. Byrne wasn't too happy to see his teammate, though. "What do you want?" he snapped. "I just wanted to know how you're doing," Coleman said. "Fine. You?" "Fine." "Well, since we're both fine," Byrne said, "I guess we've got business to do." "Yes."

Coleman ran back to his position, Byrne released the pitch, and Gil Hodges hit into an inning-ending double play.

Three years later, in the 1952 World Series, when Yankee starter Vic Raschi was struggling, Stengel whistled to second baseman Billy Martin, who dreaded to visit Raschi, who was a martinet on the mound.

"What do you want?" Raschi greeted him, irritated.

"I just wanted to know how you're doing," Martin said.

"Well, you're having enough trouble playing your own position. Don't come in here and tell me how to play mine."

Martin, with his tail between his legs, scurried back to his position at second. Later he whined to Stengel, "Don't ever send me to the mound again when Raschi's pitching. He'll punch me in the head."

So Stengel didn't get himself in trouble with the rules.

Automatic Intentional Pass?

Increasingly, there is a great deal of talk these days about speeding up the game. Enforcing the 20-second pitch rule would be one way to do it. Making a more stringent time limit on in-between-inning radio and television commercials would be the most practical way to do it. (But we know that's not going to happen!) Giving automatic intentional passes would be a third way, and it would speed up the game.

But there are at least six good reasons why an automatic intentional pass might not be good for baseball. Can you name the reasons?

* * *

One, there could be a passed ball. Two, there could be a wild pitch. Three, the backstop could step out of the batter's box too early and get called for a catcher's balk. Four, the batter could reach out and hit a pitch too close to the plate and drive it for a game-winning blow. Five, the batter could step either on the plate or over it in trying to hit the ball, and subsequently be called out. Six, the fans would be deprived of an opportunity to *boo* the pitcher! Nothing major.

An Umpire's Nightmare

Minnesota's Metrodome and Seattle's Kingdome have out-field fence ground rules that can present delicate dilemmas to umpires working in those respective parks.

Each stadium has crash paddings at the top of its fences. Suppose, on the same evening, Don Mattingly of the Yankees hits a long fly ball to right field that hits the crash padding at the Metrodome and then bounces over the fence, and Jack Clark of the Red Sox hits a deep fly ball to left field at the Kingdome that also hits the crash padding and bounces over the fence.

Are the umpires' rulings uniform in each instance?

* * *

Yes, according to the ground rules of each park, Mattingly and Clark are each credited with a ground-rule double.

* * *

Both stadiums also have outfield fences of uneven heights that join together. Suppose Mattingly's fly ball hit high up on the wall in right-center field and then bounced over the lower fence in center field. Let us suppose also that Clark's towering fly ball hit high up on the Plexiglas® in left-center field and then bounced over the lower fence in center field.

Do we once again have uniform rulings?

* * *

Yes. In the cited situations, Mattingly and Clark would each be credited with a home run.

Taking One for the Team?

Don Baylor was the career champ at getting hit by pitches. But several times during his career he was hit by a pitch and not awarded first base.

In which three situations may a batter be hit by a pitch and not be awarded first base?

*   *   *

One, if the pitch was a strike. Two, if he didn't try to avoid the pitch. And three, if the pitch follows a balk with a runner(s) on base. Rule 6.08 (b).

The Playing Manager

Don Kessinger, the last playing manager in the major leagues, removes himself from the White Sox lineup in the top half of the eighth inning, then assumes the third-base coaching reins in the bottom half of the inning.

Can he do this?

*   *   *

Yes. Here is Rule 3.03: A manager under those circumstances may continue to lead his team and may go to the coaching lines via his own directions.

Why Do Umpires Wave?

Dummy Hoy was a deaf-and-dumb outfielder for seven teams around the turn of the twentieth century. He had a .288 lifetime batting average for 14 major-league seasons, and he stole 597 career bases. He was also responsible for the umpires' raising their arms on ball-and-strike calls. Hoy couldn't hear the call, so he would turn around and look at the plate umpire. In time, the umpires started flashing him arm signals. It caught on.

Hondo

Frank Howard once hit a *bunt triple*—on the fair side of the third-base line. The opposing third basemen used to play "Hondo" five feet out on the outfield grass. This one night, Howard decided to cross up the opposition, so he dropped a bunt down the third-base line. The pitcher almost fielded the ball, but it just got by him, and in a state of frustration, he threw his glove at the rolling ball—and hit it. That's an automatic triple. One of the shortest in the history of the game!

⊙ 3 ⊙

THE OFFICIAL SCORER

Tainted Tallies

A pitcher for the Cardinals has held the Braves scoreless for eight and two-thirds innings and is trying to nail down a 1–0 shutout at Busch Stadium in St. Louis. But the Braves have dangerous Ron Gant at the plate with the bases loaded. The pitcher's two-two offering is hit right back to the mound, but the hurler's rushed throw to first baseman Andres Galarraga is wild and the ball rolls freely down the right-field line, all three runners scoring on the play.

The Braves shut down the Cardinals in the bottom of the ninth and hang on to their 3–1 lead, winning a game that but for the error they would have lost.

Since the Redbirds' pitcher's own error led to his defeat on the mound that day, are the runs that he allowed charged as earned?

*   *   *

In computing earned runs, an error by a moundsman is treated exactly the same as an error by any other fielder. Rule 10.18 (e). The runs are unearned.

Rainouts

Suppose that on the same night the Phillies in Philadelphia are leading the Cubs, 5–3, and the Yankees in New York are crushing the Red Sox, 8–1, when rain calls a halt to both games at the end of six innings. The umpires in each case wait 45 minutes before they call each game.

Is anything wrong?

* * *

Yes and no. In the National League the umpire-in-chief has to wait at least one hour and fifteen minutes before he calls the game. In the American League the umpire-in-chief has to wait only thirty minutes before he calls the contest. Rule 3.10 (c).

* * *

In the National League the Cubs could protest the game referred to above. On May 8, 1977, the Mets, who were trailing the Giants, 10–0, in the top of the seventh inning of a doubleheader, protested the game when the umpires didn't wait the required time before they cancelled play. National League President Chub Feeney upheld the protest, but the Mets finally withdrew it. They had made their point. But they didn't want the carnage to continue.

Long Enough to Win?

In this hypothetical situation, a Cincinnati Red pitcher hurls four innings of a game that is rained out after five. After four innings the Reds are leading the Astros, 9–0. The Red pitcher starts the fifth inning, but he subsequently leaves the game with two Astro runners scored, the bases loaded, and no out. The relief pitcher allows all three runners to score, but he finally slams the door on a 9–5 Red win.

Which pitcher gets credit for the victory?

* * *

The first one. The starting pitcher must hurl five complete innings for a win in any game of six or more innings. The starting pitcher, in a five-inning game, gets credit for the win if he has pitched at least four complete innings and his team not only is in the lead when he is replaced, but remains in the lead for the remainder of the game. Rule 10.19 (b).

Unfair Loss

One scorching afternoon in 1938, Phillie starting pitcher Wayne LaMaster had nothing but bad luck. With a three-one count on Cub lead-off batter Stan Hack, he hurt his arm and had to be relieved. The Philadelphia relief pitcher came into the game and promptly walked Hack, the free pass being credited to LaMaster's record. Hack came around to score the first of 21 runs that Chicago scored that day. The Phillies scored two times.

* * *

Normally, the relief pitcher would get eight warm-up throws. But when there is an injury and the reliever has not had time to warm up, the umpire will tell him, "You can take as many pitches as you want." Rule 8.03.

Who was the losing pitcher?

* * *

LaMaster, though he did not face even one complete batter, was charged with the loss, because he was credited with the first Cub run, scored before he took the mound. And the Phillies never tied the score or took the lead in his absence.

Relief Pitcher Hurled Shutout

Suppose Bob Turley of the 1959 Yankees relieves Don Larsen with the bases loaded and no out, in the first inning, and he goes on to retire the side without allowing a run en route to a 4–0 victory.

Does he get credit for a shutout?

* * *

Yes. Rule 10.19 (f) reads: "No pitcher shall be credited with pitching a shutout unless he pitches the complete game, or unless he enters the game with none out before the opposing team has scored in the first inning, puts out the side without a run scoring and pitches all the rest of the game."

* * *

In our first *Baseball Brain Teaser* book, we pointed out that Ernie Shore of the Red Sox relieved Babe Ruth in the first inning of a game in 1917. Ray Morgan of the Senators had walked, and was on first base with no out. Ruth had been ejected by the home-plate umpire when he blasphemously protested the fourth-ball call to Morgan. With Shore pitching, Morgan was thrown out attempting to steal, and Shore went on to retire 26 consecutive batters in a game that went into the record books as a perfect game.

A special committee, headed by Commissioner Fay Vincent, ruled in the summer of 1991 that Shore couldn't have pitched a perfect game, because Morgan had reached base for the Senators in the game, so they removed Shore's name from the list of "perfect-game" pitchers.

But he is still credited with a shutout—in relief!

Hard-Luck Pitcher

The Oakland A's, the champions of the Western Division, are playing the Toronto Blue Jays, the winners of the Eastern Division. It is the seventh game of the pennant series.

In the top of the second inning, Toronto takes a 2–0 lead off Oakland's starting pitcher, Bob Welch. Oakland manager Tony LaRussa goes to his bullpen, bringing in Rick Honeycutt with one out and two men on base. During his two-and-two-thirds inning stint, Honeycutt bars the door on the Blue Jays, shutting them down on two hits and one walk, while the A's rebound to take a 3–2 lead.

Jimmy Key then comes on for Oakland and sets down Toronto with no runs and just one hit in five innings of pitching. The A's win the game, 5–2, and the pennant, 4–3.

Honeycutt pitched effectively and was the pitcher of record when the A's took the lead that they never relinquished. But Key was utterly awesome.

To whom do you give the win?

*   *   *

That is a debatable point. The official scorer will be guided by Rule 10.19 (c)(4), which reads, "The winning relief pitcher shall be the one who is the pitcher of record when his team assumes the lead and maintains it to the finish of the game. EXCEPTION: Do not credit a victory to a relief pitcher who is ineffective in a brief appearance, when a succeeding relief pitcher pitches effectively in helping his team maintain the lead. In such cases, credit the succeeding relief pitcher with the victory."

*   *   *

The wording in the above rule would seem to indicate that Honeycutt, the pitcher of record who hurled effectively, would get the win. But an official scorer's ruling in the final game of the 1947 World Series, between the

Brooklyn Dodgers and the Yankees, contradicts that conclusion.

Put Bill Bevens and the Yankees in the place of Rick Honeycutt and the A's, and place Joe Page in the role of Key, and you've got a precisely similar situation. But in 1947 the scorer gave the victory to Page, who came into the game with a 3–2 lead and left it with a 5–2 win.

The decision was just the last chapter in a full season of poor luck for Bevens. From 1944 to 1946 he posted win-loss records of 4–1, 13–9, and 16–13. But in 1947, on a pennant-winning club, he logged a sub-par 7–13 mark.

In the fourth game of the World Series, he started and became the pitcher who had come the closest to spinning a no-hitter in a Fall Classic contest. After eight and two-thirds innings, he had pitched scoreless ball, but he was clinging precariously to a 2–1 lead. Brooklyn had runners on first and second with two out when pinch-hitter Harry "Cookie" Lavagetto hit a game-winning double off the right field wall in the bottom of the ninth inning.

Bevens pitched one more time in the Series, the Game Seven alluded to above. And in that game, although he pitched brilliantly while giving his teammates a chance to get back in the game, a victory eluded him once more. It was the last time he had an opportunity to pick up a win in the majors. The following spring, he came down with a sore arm, and he never again pitched in the major leagues.

Who Gets the Save?

During the 1992 season, Jeff Reardon of the Red Sox broke Rollie Fingers' former all-time career record for saves (341).

In one of his games during the 1992 campaign, with Boston leading its opposition, 6–3, he came to the mound with two runners on base and two out in the top half of the ninth inning. On one pitch he retired the batter to nail down a victory for the BoSox.

Did he get credited with a save?

* * *

Yes, he did. In order to qualify for a save, the relief pitcher must satisfy *one* of the following three conditions:

1) His team must have been leading by no more than three runs—and he must have pitched effectively—when he entered the game; or

2) When he entered the game, the tying run must have been on base, on deck, or at bat; or

3) He must have effectively pitched three or more innings. Rule 10.20.

Reardon qualified under rules one and two.

* * *

In another late-season game in 1992, Dennis Eckersley of the Oakland A's picked up a save under similar circumstances. He was embarrassed, though. The "save" was too cheap, he said.

Everything's relative. In 1973, for example, a relief pitcher would have been credited with a save for "saving" a 15–3 rout.

Down to the Wire

Dennis Eckersley, in his first five years with the Oakland A's (1987–91), posted ERA marks of 3.03, 2.35, 1.56, 0.61, and 2.96.

Did he ever win an ERA title?

* * *

No. He never during that period pitched the required number of innings in order to qualify for the title. According to an amendment to the official baseball rules in 1951, a pitcher must hurl a total of at least one inning for every scheduled game (162 today) to be eligible as the league leader. Before 1951, he had to hurl at least 10 complete games and at least 100 innings.

Eckersley has neither completed a game in his stay with the A's nor pitched more than 116 innings in a season. He didn't qualify—he wasn't pitching before the 1951 amendment and never in one season pitched 162 innings.

* * *

Bill Stafford of the 1961 Yankees, in his first full season in the majors, posted a 14–9 win-loss record with a 2.68 ERA in 195 innings of pitching. He almost won the ERA title. But Dick Donovan of the White Sox, who was two innings shy of the minimum number of 162 going into the final game of the season, pitched eight and two-thirds innings of scoreless ball to win the title with a mark of 2.40.

That same day, Stafford finished up the season in championship form, too. He pitched a 1–0 shutout against pitching counterpart Tracy Stallard of the Red Sox. The only run of the game scored on Roger Maris' record 61st home run in a season.

Change of Error

Early in the 1992 season, in a game between the visiting Oakland A's and the Yankees, New York's Mike Gallego attempted to steal second base in the first inning. Catcher Terry Steinbach released a skip-hop throw to shortstop Mike Borders, Gallego's slide created a cloud of dust, and the second-base umpire called the runner out.

When the dust had cleared, though, the ball was rolling free on the ground, and the umpire reversed his call, ruling Gallego safe.

Does the official scorer award an error on the play?

* * *

Initially, he did. He gave Borders an error, and he didn't give Gallego a stolen base. The scorer's reasoning was that since the umpire initially called the runner out and then changed his decision, someone had to be charged with an error on the play.

But a catcher can't be charged with an error on an attempted steal unless his action contributes to an additional advance by the runner on the play (from second to third, let us say). Rule 10.14 (a). The only other defensive player to whom an error could have been awarded was Borders. If the A's shortstop had cleanly handled Steinbach's throw, and Gallego's contact had subsequently knocked the ball out of his glove, then the error would have been awarded justifiably. But the instant replay didn't indicate that there had been possession on Borders' part.

In a case like this one, the official scorer will *usually* question the player to whom the error was awarded after the game. Wisely, this umpire did. Borders said that he never had clean possession of the ball.

Since a player doesn't usually receive an error for a throw that arrives on a short hop, Borders' "error" was removed, and Gallego was credited with a stolen base.

A Streaky Subject

Two players have hit safely in a record 12 consecutive at-bats: Mike "Pinky" Higgins of the 1938 Red Sox and Walt "Moose" Dropo of the 1952 Tigers.

Suppose, for the sake of debate, Higgins, within his streak, was walked twice and the recipient of one defensive interference call. Would his streak have been terminated?

* * *

No.

* * *

Suppose Dropo, within his streak, got hit by a pitch, hit a sacrifice fly, and laid down a sacrifice bunt. Would his streak end?

* * *

Yes. If he had just gotten hit by a pitch and laid down a sacrifice bunt, the streak would still be intact. However, a sacrifice fly does terminate a hitting streak. Rule 10.24 (a).

* * *

Ted Williams of the 1957 Red Sox is a good example of the above rule. In that year he reached base a record 16 consecutive times. During that streak he stroked two singles, banged four home runs, received nine bases on balls, and got hit by one pitch. The walks and hit-by-pitch did not terminate his streak, but a sac-fly did not count as a hit.

Is Sacrifice an At-Bat?

Ken Griffey of the host Mariners is on third base with no out in a 3–3 game with the Oakland A's. Kevin Mitchell, the Mariners batter, hits a long fly ball that center fielder Willie Wilson tracks down and catches near the fence in left-center, Griffey scoring on the play.

Does Mitchell get an RBI, exempting him from an at-bat?

*   *   *

Yes, he does.

*   *   *

Has the present rule always been in effect?

*   *   *

No, it hasn't. It came into effect, in its present form, in 1908. Eighteen years later (1926), the sacrifice fly rule was amended so that a batter was charged with no at-bat if any baserunner advanced a base on a "fly ball." In 1931, five years later, the sacrifice fly rule went out of effect until 1939, when it was reinstated in its initial form (no at-bat when runner moves up) for just one year. There was no sacrifice fly rule from 1939 until 1954, when it was reintroduced in its present form.

*   *   *

Baseball is usually a constant game. But not the sacrifice fly rule, which has affected career batting averages. For example, Joe DiMaggio (1936–51) played only one year with the rule in effect. Hank Aaron (1954–76), on the other hand, played his entire career with the rule in effect.

Lifetime, DiMaggio batted .325; Aaron, .305.

To Err Is Human

With one out, Willie Randolph on first base, and the Mets leading the Braves, 6–5, in the bottom of the seventh inning, Tom Glavine is pitching to Howard Johnson with a two-one count. As Randolph breaks for second on the pitch, Johnson swings through a fastball, but the pitch gets by the Brave backstop and rolls all the way to the screen. Randolph continues to third on the play.

Does Randolph get a stolen base? What about the catcher? Does he get charged with a passed ball?

* * *

Randolph is credited with a stolen base, and the catcher receives a passed ball. Rule 10.08 (a) EXCEPTION.

* * *

Let's slightly change the scenario. Suppose Randolph advances only to second on the play. What is the answer to the above two questions?

* * *

Randolph still gets credit for a stolen base, but the catcher is not charged with an error. Rule 10.08 (a). When the baserunner breaks for the advance base before the pitcher throws to the plate, a stolen base is credited and the pitch is recorded as a wild pitch or a passed ball. A stolen base *and* a wild pitch or a passed ball are recorded if the runner is able to advance two bases on the play.

* * *

In a 1971 game between the Giants and the host Astros, this play occurred. Houston catcher Johnny Edwards was on third base in a close game. Manager Preston Gomez flashed the suicide squeeze sign, Edwards took off for the plate before the pitcher's release, and Don Wilson squared to bunt. But Wilson missed the pitch, as did the Giant catcher, and Edwards scored standing up. The official scorer correctly ruled the play a stolen base.

But National League President Chub Feeney was in attendance that night, and he disagreed with the ruling. He thought that the catcher should be charged with a passed ball. The official scorer vindicated himself by showing Feeney Rule 10.08 (a), but Feeney was still not convinced. He discussed the matter with the rules committee, but the rule remains the same today.

The Batter Couldn't Strike Out

Let us suppose that in the 1954 World Series, between the Indians and the Giants, when pinch-hitter deluxe James "Dusty" Rhodes substituted at-bat for Monte Irvin that Irvin had a count of three balls and two strikes on him, when Rhodes proceeded to strike out.

Would Irvin or Rhodes be charged with the strikeout?

*   *   *

Irvin. When the batter leaves the game with two strikes against him, and the substitute batter completes a strikeout, charge the strikeout and the time at-bat to the first batter. If the substitute batter completes the time at-bat in any other manner, including a base on balls, score the action as having been that of the substitute batter. Rule 10.17 (d).

Actually, what happened in the above example of the 1954 World Series, in which the Giants swept the Indians in four games, is that Rhodes pinch-hit for Irvin three times, batting safely each time. He did not interrupt any at-bats, however. Previously, in the 1951 World Series, in which the Yankees defeated the Giants in seven games, Irvin paced the Polo Grounders with 11 hits in 24 at-bats for a .458 average. *Tempus fugit!*

In Gehrig's Footsteps

If Cal Ripken plays in every game for the next four years, he will break Lou Gehrig's record of playing in 2,130 consecutive games.

Undoubtedly, during that time span, Ripken will have days when he just doesn't have the energy to perform at his peak. He may be injured, ill, or just plain fatigued. Perhaps his manager will want to give him a break, also.

Without terminating his streak, can he—

1. Play just one-half an inning on defense before leaving the game?

2. Complete just one at-bat by reaching base or being put out before leaving the game?

3. Pinch-run for his only appearance in the game?

4. Be ejected by an umpire?

Answers: 1. Yes. 2. Yes. 3. No. Pinch-running alone is not sufficient to extend a consecutive-game playing streak. 4. Yes. Ejection will not break the sequence. Rule 10.24 (c).

Infield Fly Bounce

The Twins, in a game against the visiting Royals, have Chuck Knoblauch on second base, Phil Gagne on first, and Shane Mack at the plate with one out in the fifth inning.

On Kevin Appier's first pitch, Mack hits a towering pop fly towards the Royal shortstop. The second-base umpire immediately calls the infield-fly rule. But the Kansas City shortstop has difficulty with the high sky, and he staggers under the ball. Knoblauch prepares to advance if the ball rolls free. The ball falls untouched to the ground, near the embarrassed shortstop, but it takes a freak hop, and it hits Knoblauch as he hurries back to second.

Mack, of course, is out on the infield-fly rule for the second out of the inning. But two questions remain: Is Knoblauch out, because he has been hit by a fair batted ball which has not been touched by a fielder, and does Mack get credit for a hit, because his batted ball hit a runner in fair territory?

* * *

Knoblauch is out. He becomes the third out of the inning. Rule 7.08 (f). Mack does not get credit for a hit. The official scorer does not score a hit when a runner is called out for having been touched by an infield fly. Rule 10.05 (e) EXCEPTION.

Don't Catch It!

In the bottom of the ninth inning, in a game between the Cardinals and the host Pirates, Andy Van Slyke, who represents the game-winning run, is at third base with one out. Batter Barry Bonds hits a long foul fly ball down the left-field line. The ball is hit deep enough to score the winning run. The Redbird leftfielder knows this, so he deliberately lets the ball fall untouched to the ground.

Does he receive an error on this play?

* * *

No. An error shall not be charged against any fielder who permits a foul fly to fall safe with a runner on third base before two are out, if in the scorer's judgment the fielder deliberately refuses the catch in order that the runner on third shall not score after the catch. Rule 10.14 (e).

"The F.B.I. told us to have these guys change numbers. What don't you believe?"

Billy Was Expendable

Just before the Yankees traveled to Boston for a key series in 1950, Phil Rizzuto received a letter, saying that he, Johnny Mize, Yogi Berra, and Hank Bauer would be shot if they played in the Red Sox series. Rizzuto handed the letter over to manager Casey Stengel, who delivered it to the FBI. Then Casey acted in the Yankees' best interests. He had Rizzuto and Billy Martin switch uniform numbers. Rizzuto wore Martin's number "1" and Martin wore Rizzuto's number "10."

In Game One of the series, Rizzuto batted first and Martin eighth. Rizzuto singled to left field in his first trip to the plate. After he reached first base, Red Sox coach Earle Combs approached the first-base umpire and said that Rizzuto, since he was not wearing the number that was recorded on the lineup card, should be called out for batting out of order.

Was he?

* * *

While Rizzuto was in technical violation of the rule, there was no penalty. The batting-out-of-order rule requires only that the name be in the proper batting order. Regardless of number, the name of the player batting must be correct or the batting-out-of-order penalty will be imposed. Rule 6.07.

Heady Play in a Rundown

In a game between the Brewers and the host Red Sox, Milwaukee has Robin Yount on second base and Paul Molitor on first base with two out in the top of the sixth inning.

The Boston pitcher picks up Molitor, who is too far off first base, and the Brewer infielder gets caught up in a rundown between first baseman Carlos Quintana and shortstop Jody Reed. After several exchanges of the ball by the Red Sox infielders, Molitor manages to make his way safely back to first base. In the meantime, Yount advances to third on the play.

Does Yount get credit for a stolen base?

* * *

Yes. If a runner advances while another runner, attempting to steal, evades being put out in a rundown play and returns safely, without the aid of an error, to the base he originally occupied, credit a stolen base to the runner who advances. Rule 10.08 (c).

* * *

In a 1955 game between the Oakland A's and the Yankees, Dave Winfield got hung up between third and home when a suicide squeeze backfired. Winfield managed to evade the tag of A's pitcher, Tommy John, however, and he slid across home plate with an unexpected Yankee run. He got credit for a stolen base on the play.

Misuse of Mask

Mike Scioscia, the longtime catcher for the Los Angeles Dodgers, had a "Murphy's Law" year in 1992. If anything could go wrong, it did. Take the following play, for example.

The host San Diego Padres are trailing the Los Angeles Dodgers in the bottom of the eighth inning, 3–2, when San Diego rallies. With Tony Fernandez on second base and two out, Tony Gwynn singles to right field to tie the score, and on the throw to the plate, he advances to second base.

In the meantime, Scioscia bobbles the skip throw from the outfield, and then reaches out with his right hand—which holds his mask—and scoops up the free ball into his mitt.

Instantaneously, San Diego manager Greg Riddoch charges home plate and demands that his runner score from second base on Scioscia's catcher's interference.

Does the Padre pilot have a valid point?

*   *   *

Yes, he does. Each runner, including the batter-runner, may without liability to be put out, advance two bases, if a fielder deliberately touches a thrown ball with his cap, mask, or any part of his uniform detached from its proper place on his person. The ball is in play. Rule 7.04 (d).

A similar-type play was called against Mike Heath, when he was catching for the Tigers in the late 1980s. On a late throw from the outfield to the plate, the ball took a bad bounce to Heath's right, and he reached out with the mask in his right hand and caught it. The batter-runner, who had reached second base on the throw to the plate, was allowed to score.

Around the Horn

Gary Gaetti, during the years when he was the third baseman for the Twins, initiated a couple of triple plays from third to second to first base.

Suppose that one night he had the opportunity of starting a third triple play. Playing close to the third-base bag with no out and the bases loaded, he cleanly fielded the batter's hard-hit smash, stepped on the base, threw to the second baseman for the second out, and watched in amazement as the pivot man, with the batter-runner barely out of the batter's box, threw the ball wildly past first baseman Kent Hrbek. The runner from third scored and the batter-runner stayed at first base on the play.

The second baseman had a simple play to make to get his team out of a tough situation. The fact that he didn't execute an elementary play allowed the opposition to score at least one run and keep its inning alive. Does the second baseman get an error on the play?

* * *

He does not. No error shall be charged against any fielder when he makes a wild throw in attempting to complete a double or triple play, unless such wild throw enables any runner to advance beyond the base he would have reached had the throw not been wild. Rule 10.14 (c).

◉ 4 ◉

BASEBALL LAFFES
AND GAFFES

The Wrong Club

George Strickland once took a very low pitch, in his opinion, which the umpire called strike two. Strickland didn't say anything, but he started to walk back to the dugout.

"Heh, where are you going?" protested the umpire. "That's only strike two."

"I know," said Strickland, "but I brought the wrong club up to the plate. I'm going back to get my wedge."

Haste Makes Waste

When Hank Greenberg was the general manager of the Indians, he was perplexed one day when he received an unsigned contract in the mail from a veteran player. Greenberg rushed off a terse wire to the player: "In your haste to agree to terms, you forgot to sign the contract."

He received a laconic note in reply: "In your haste to give me a big raise, you inserted the wrong figure."

A Better Way to Earn a Living

Jocko Conlan became a major-league umpire under extraordinary circumstances in between innings of a game between the White Sox and the Browns. Conlan was playing for the White Sox when one of the base umpires fainted because of heat exhaustion, and no other umpires were on hand. The two clubs agreed that Conlan, as a veteran player, was the best choice to umpire—and he could leave his White Sox uniform on!

Actually, Conlan had decided to become an umpire several months before that hot and humid day. One day he hit a ground ball to deep short, and he busted his gut running down the line to beat the throw.

As he neared the base, he noticed that the umpire there, Clarence "Brick" Owen, was standing with his hands in his pockets and his right thumb dangling in public view. As Conlan got to the base, Owen wiggled him out.

The exasperated Conlan said to Owen, "I've got to run and grunt and sweat, and that's all there is to your job, that little wiggle?" Owen nodded and smiled. From that moment, Conlan knew what he was going to do for the rest of his working life.

Quick Comeback

Dusty Boggess, the umpire, always had a quick comeback remark on the field. One day, in his first year of umpiring, Boggess called Clyde McCullough of the Pirates out on a borderline pitch.

McCullough walked away, quietly saying, "You missed it, Dusty. The pitch was low."

"For twenty years as a player, I thought so, too, Mac," Boggess replied. "But it's a strike. That's why I got out of playing and into umpiring."

"Why can't you wear a wrist watch like everyone else?"

Yogi's Award

Umpire Larry Napp recalls the night that he and Yogi Berra were walking out of Toots Shor's restaurant together. Yogi was carrying a big clock that he had just received at the banquet.

Suddenly a drunk bumped into Yogi, who quickly said, "Excuse me."

The drunk looked at Yogi incoherently and said, "Why can't you wear a wristwatch like everyone else?"

A Very Clean Plate

One day during the early 1920s the plate umpire, Tommy Connolly, called a strike on Yankee second baseman Aaron Ward, and the infielder took off his hat and dusted off the plate while the arbiter gritted his teeth.

On the next pitch from Red Faber of the White Sox, Connolly called an inside pitch a ball, and the hurler screamed at the umpire while Ray Schalk, his catcher, doffed his hat and cleaned the plate.

On the following pitch, Ward looked bad as he struck out swinging on a forkball (split fastball).

Delightedly, Connolly took off his cap and dusted off the plate.

The Unintentional Walk

Billy Meyer, when he was the manager of the Pirates from 1948 to 1952, used to like to put on the steal-of-home sign when there were two out, the bases loaded, and a three-one count on the batter.

His thinking was that the pitcher would become so flustered that he would deliberately throw the ball outside or up-and-in for a ball. In either case it would be ball four, forcing in a run.

Sometimes the umpire would forget the count, too. Invariably, he would call the runner out, and then when he realized that the pitch was ball four, forcing home this runner, he would, embarrassed, reverse his call.

The Radio Pitch

One night Max Surkont of the Boston Braves was stifling the Pirate lineup when manager Billy Meyer sent up George "Catfish" Metkovich to pinch-hit in the late innings. Metkovich had batted against Surkont in the Pacific Coast League the year before.

But Metkovich took three straight strikes before gently placing his bat back in the rack.

The bench was suddenly silent. Metkovich finally broke the silence with an enigmatic statement: "He threw me his radio pitch."

"Radio pitch?" questioned rookie Dick Groat.

"Yeah, you can hear it but you can't see it."

You Really Meant It?

When Fred Haney was the manager of the Pirates (1953 to 1955), he gave one of his players the steal sign three different times during the same at-bat, and the player never ran.

On all three pitches Brooklyn Dodger catcher Roy Campanella, who was certain that he had read the sign, called for a pitch-out. After the third ball, however, he wasn't so sure.

In fact, Haney, who was giving the signs, wasn't absolutely certain that he was giving the right sign, either. After the runner came in for the next Pittsburgh at-bat, Haney said, "Did you get the steal sign?"

The player said, "Yeah."

"I gave it to you three times. Why didn't you run?"

"I didn't think you meant it."

The Car-Wash Staff

When Billy Martin was managing the Oakland A's in 1980, virtually every pitcher on his 10-man staff was suspected of throwing a spitball.

Broadcaster Joe Garagiola mused one day, "The Oakland pitching staff must warm up in a car wash."

Pitching His Own Game

One day Joe Garagiola of the Cardinals was catching relief pitcher Ted Wilks in a game against the Brooklyn Dodgers. Duke Snider was the batter. He was a good fastball hitter. So naturally Garagiola signalled for a curveball, and Wilks threw a fastball. Strike one.

Then Garagiola figured Snider would be looking for a fastball, so he gave the sign for a curve. Once again Wilks threw a fastball, this time for a swinging strike. Garagiola now thought they would waste a curveball, down and away. For the third straight time Wilks threw a fastball, right down the middle of the plate. Snider looked at it for strike three.

When Garagiola went out to the mound to check the signals, Wilks said, "I'm sorry. I must have forgot." Garagiola came back to the plate shaking his head.

Plate umpire Larry Goetz said to him, "I knew you had him (Snider), because obviously you didn't know what was coming, and I certainly didn't know what was coming, so Duke couldn't have known what was coming, either."

Favorite Umpire

One night George Brett of the Royals sidled up to Ron Luciano at third base and said, "I wouldn't want you to spread this around, but you're my favorite umpire."

Umpires are human, too, and they have feelings just like anyone else, and to put it mildly Luciano felt 10 feet tall. He couldn't wait until after the game, when he could share the information with his crew.

But he was beaten to the punch. Davey Phillips said somewhat innocently, "You know what George Brett told me tonight? He said that I was his favorite umpire."

"He tells that to every umpire," Bill Haller said, laughing as he listed a long list of arbiters who had made the same confession as Phillips.

Luciano suddenly felt six feet tall. "Yeah, Davey," he added somewhat lamely. "Didn't you know that?"

Master of the One-Liners

Craig Nettles, when he was playing with the Yankees in the 1970s and 1980s, was the master of the one-liners.

One day he put his Yankee experiences in perspective. "When I was young, I wanted either to play baseball or join a circus. I've been lucky. With the Yankees, I've gotten the opportunity to do both."

*   *   *

One night he was playing in a game in which Carl Yastrzemski of the Red Sox got his 3,000th career hit. The game was interrupted while fans stormed onto the field, photographers took countless pictures, the governor of Massachusetts made a speech, and Red Sox officials gave him both the ball and first base. Finally Nettles ambled up to the third-base umpire and said, "Jeez, it was only a single."

I Shall Return

One of the first places General Douglas MacArthur visited upon his return from Korea was the Polo Grounds.

"It's great to be here," he said. "There are no sounds more soothing to the ear than the bat against glove, glove against ball, the call of hot peanuts and cold beer, and the fans booing the umpire."

INDEX

126